Living Well with Emphysema and Bronchitis

Living Well with Emphysema and Bronchitis

A Handbook for Everyone with Chronic Obstructive Pulmonary Disease

Myra B. Shayevitz, M.D., F.C.C.P.
Berton R. Shayevitz, M.D.

DOUBLEDAY & COMPANY, INC.
GARDEN CITY, NEW YORK

Line drawings by Phillip Jones

Library of Congress Cataloging in Publication Data

Shayevitz, Myra B., 1934–
   Living well with emphysema and bronchitis.

   Bibliography: p. 205
   Includes index.
   1. Emphysema—Patients—Rehabilitation—Handbooks,
manuals, etc. 2. Bronchitis—Patients—Rehabilitation—
Handbooks, manuals, etc. I. Shayevitz, Berton R.,
1931–   . II. Title.
RC776.E5S5   1985   616.2'48   84–18836
ISBN 0-385-19438-2

616.2

B6636

We dedicate this book to all our patients
and those who love them

Acknowledgments

A very special note of thanks to James R. McCormick, M.D., F.C.C.P., Associate Professor of Medicine, Medical College of Georgia, and Chief of Pulmonary Section and Director of Pulmonary Immunology Research, Veterans Administration Medical Center, Augusta, Georgia, who critically reviewed the entire manuscript with such care.

We are grateful to William Rohan, Ph.D., Norman Tallent, Ph.D., Mary O. Rodowicz, R.D., Joanne Carney, R.D., Bernard Langlais, C.R.T. supervisor of respiratory therapy, Sandra O'Donnell, M.A., Katherine Krusas, R.N., Robert Malikin, M.S.W., and Nan and John Winninger, for reviewing portions of our manuscript.

Our own program was in large part inspired by the ideas of the farseeing Dr. Thomas L. Petty, M.D., F.C.C.P., Professor of Medicine, Co-Head, Division of Pulmonary Sciences, University of Colorado Medical Center, Director, Webb-Waring Lung Institute, Denver, Colorado, the pioneer in the field of pulmonary rehabilitation. We thank Dr. Petty for composing the Foreword.

Other leaders in the field of pulmonary medicine who have contributed greatly to our education are Sanford Chodosh, M.D., F.C.C.P., Director of the Sputum Laboratory, Boston City Hospital;

David Frederick, M.D., Assistant Professor of Medicine, University of Connecticut Medical School; John E. Hodgkin, M.D., F.C.C.P., Clinical Professor of Medicine, University of California at Davis, Medical Director, Center for Health Promotion and Rehabilitation, St. Helena, California; John N. Landis, M.D., F.C.C.P., Clinical Associate Professor of Medicine, Tufts University School of Medicine, Boston, Massachusetts; Chief, Pulmonary Service, Baystate Medical Center, Springfield, Massachusetts; Howard M. Kravetz, M.D., F.C.C.P., Associate Internal Medicine, University of Arizona College of Medicine, Tucson, Arizona; Chief, Mountain Air Rehabilitation Center for Health, Yavapai Regional Medical Center, Prescott, Arizona; and Howard Turner, M.D., F.C.C.P., former Chief, Pulmonary Service, Baystate Medical Center, Springfield, Massachusetts.

A very special thanks to the eminent authority and teacher Gordon L. Snider, M.D., F.C.C.P., Professor of Medicine, Boston University Medical School, for critically reading this book.

We thank the entire staff of the Acute Care Medical Service, Veterans Administration Medical Center, Northampton, Massachusetts.

George Kraker, R.C.P.T., helped design the illustrations.

Gail Beaudoin prepared the original table of contents, and Joan Sorgi prepared the presentation illustrations. Jessie Hunt, Sadie Church, and Rose Baker tested and revised recipes.

Judy Stark typed the entire manuscript with outstanding patience and competence.

Adelaide and Zal Saltman ensured the prompt arrival of the original manuscript to the publisher.

A special note of thanks to Sidney and Helen Radner for their expertise on Houdini and their valued opinions.

We especially wish to thank Antonios P. Stathatos, M.D., Chief, Medical Service, Veterans Administration Medical Center, Northampton, Massachusetts, who inspired our best efforts. In fact, the staff and administration of the Veterans Administration Medical Center in Northampton have helped us in many ways and have provided an environment for professional growth.

Frank Katch, Ph.D., Chairman of the Exercise Science Department, University of Massachusetts, Amherst, Massachusetts, showed us the magic and the power of scientific exercise and reviewed Chapter 4, "Body Business," and Chapter 5, "Exercise."

Sushma Palmer, D.Sc., Executive Director, Food and Nutrition Board, National Research Council, also critically reviewed Chapter 4, "Body Business."

We thank Charles H. Nightingale, Ph.D., Director, Department of Pharmacy Services, Hartford Hospital, Hartford, Connecticut; Research Professor, University of Connecticut School of Pharmacy, and his staff for reviewing the prescribed medications chart.

Cheryl Vitale, R.R.T., provided valuable information on traveling with oxygen.

Our special thanks to our agent, Ms. Ruth Wreschner of New York City.

Another note of special thanks to our editors at Doubleday, Doreen DeFlorio and Jean Anne Vincent, our illustrator, Phil Jones, and our art director, Diana Klemin.

Contents

Foreword

I was delighted to see this book written by two long-term friends. The reason for my delight is the fact that the public is clamoring for knowledge about how to cope with emphysema and bronchitis and how to get on with living. Myra and Bert Shayevitz have done a magnificent job in explaining the problems of chronic obstructive pulmonary disease (COPD) in a manner highly understandable to those who suffer from the disease and to their families. I was pleased about the reference to my own work in pulmonary rehabilitation. In the mid-sixties, Louise Nett and I decided that something had to be done for emphysema victims other than to tell them to go home and not overdo. Stimulated by the challenge of improving the life and happiness of people with emphysema, we devoted a substantial part of our professional lives to making things better for these patients and their families. In fact, we wrote two books ourselves *(For Those Who Live and Breathe,* C.C. Thomas, 1967, and *Enjoying Life with Emphysema,* Lea & Febiger, 1984). Alas, these two books never reached the public in sufficient numbers to have the impact that we hoped.

Fortunately, Doubleday has seen the wisdom of publishing and distributing this new book, which will be of interest to all patients suffering from emphysema, chronic bronchitis, or even related asthma, and certainly to their families. Indeed, physicians, nurses, respiratory therapists, and home-care providers would do well to consider the wisdom and advice in this highly readable book. Coping with frustration and in general dealing with problems of sexuality, developing a partnership with the physician and other care-givers, and getting on with the business of living in spite of emphysema and bronchitis is a huge challenge. Those who are faced with the burdens of COPD should consider coping with it an adventure, and they will be well guided by this book.

THOMAS L. PETTY, M.D., F.C.C.P.
Director, Webb-Waring Lung Institute, Denver, Colorado
Co-Head, Division of Pulmonary Sciences, University of Colorado Medical Center, Denver
Professor of Medicine, University of Colorado, Denver

Introduction

Have you given up a great deal in life because of chronic bronchitis, emphysema, or chronic asthma, also known as chronic obstructive pulmonary disease, or COPD? Do you sit idly most of the day, bored? If you work, is it getting harder and harder? Do you spend a good portion of the day afraid—not understanding your disease or what to do about it? If this is so, we say, "Enough!" You can live a full life in spite of COPD. In fact, you can "live well" with a wide range of activities. Chances are you can exercise actively, eat well, have sex, participate in recreational activities, and enjoy life again.

If you are using this book in conjunction with an established pulmonary rehabilitation program, you are very fortunate indeed, for pulmonary rehabilitation centers can improve functioning by a full 50 percent, and this book should provide valuable supplemental guidance and information.

If not, use this book in conjunction with your own physician to create your own individual rehabilitation program.

Read carefully and thoughtfully. You are about to become a member of your own health care team.

AUTHORS' NOTES: For clarity's sake we have shown men in all illustrations and described doctors as he and nurses as she. We realize and hope you do, too, that in each case the roles might be reversed.

We assume in each chapter (except that on sex) that you are alone and must function entirely independently. If, however, you are lucky enough to have a partner to assist you, use your new knowledge to become a true helpmate.

Although we will remind you of this from time to time throughout the book, please remember that all the suggestions herein are subject to your doctor's approval.

Living Well with Emphysema and Bronchitis

1

COPD: Chronic Bronchitis, Emphysema, and Chronic Asthma Explained

Have you been diagnosed as having COPD—chronic bronchitis, emphysema, or chronic asthma?

Have you a full understanding of these diseases and their relationship to each other?

Do you want to know exactly what these terms mean and have a full comprehension of their effect on you and your family? If so, read on.

COPD, an abbreviation for chronic obstructive pulmonary disease, usually refers to chronic bronchitis and emphysema, which affect twenty-five million persons in the United States and comprise the fastest-growing health problem in this country. Chronic bronchitis and emphysema are responsible for at least fifty thousand deaths a year in the United States alone. The death rate is rising, apparently associated with an increase in cigarette consumption and perhaps air pollution. In males over the age of forty, COPD is second only to coronary disease as a cause of disability. With the increase in the incidence of smoking among females in the past few years has come a concomitant increase in deaths from COPD in women. Moreover, dying is only part of the problem. It is the long years of disability, joblessness, loss of income, depression, repeated hospitalization, loss of family and the normal activities which give life meaning (such as recreation, sex, and work) that make chronic bronchitis and emphysema frightening problems.

At least six million people in the United States are affected by asthma, a disease which frequently begins in childhood but which may have its onset quite late in life. Asthma is not caused by smoking cigarettes. Asthma beginning early in life is usually associated with an allergy and tends to disappear with adulthood, while the asthma of adults is frequently chronic, nonallergenic in nature, and followed by permanent remission in less than 25 percent of cases. Although the causes of chronic bronchitis, emphysema, and asthma are completely different, the symptoms, medications, problems, and sometimes the lifelong course are similar. In addition, these diseases often coexist in the same person, with each one contributing to the affected individual's symptoms. Before we describe the individual disorders and their similarities, we need to study some basic anatomy and physiology. One thing is certain: You owe it to yourself, to the one life on earth that you have, to know all about these diseases.

ANATOMY AND PHYSIOLOGY LESSONS

Air, smoke, germs, allergens and pollutants pass from the nose and mouth into a large central duct called the *trachea*. The trachea branches into smaller ducts, the *bronchi* and *bronchioles*, which lead to the *alveoli* (Fig. 1). These latter are the air sacs, tiny, delicate, balloonlike structures composed of blood vessels (capillaries) supported by connecting tissue and enclosed in a gossamer-thin membrane. The respiratory system is like a tree: The trachea is the trunk, the bronchi and bronchioles are the branches. This is known as the bronchial tree, a term we'll use from now on. The alveoli are the leaves. The blood vessels of the alveoli carry the red blood cells, which pick up oxygen and transport it to the rest of the body. Carbon dioxide, a cellular waste product, is released to the alveoli from the bloodstream and exhaled. The tiny alveoli, supported by a framework of delicate elastic fibers, give the lung a very distensible quality

Fig. 2) Nonsmokers' Army. Ciliated cells lining the airway in a normal lung, standing closely at attention. Artist's rendition adapted from an actual photomicrograph of a lung magnified 4,000. *American Lung Association Bulletin* Vol 64 No 10 (December 1978): 8.

now contains white blood cells (polymorphonuclear leukocytes, hereafter referred to as *PMN*s), defense cells to fight off the infecting organisms by engulfing them. When the bacteria win, the infection becomes deep enough to cause actual destruction of the bronchial wall. Scar tissue replaces the fine cells lining the bronchial tree, and scars give rise to areas of narrowing. Some bronchioles become totally obliterated. *Bronchospasm,* or tightening of the muscles of the bronchial tree, occurs (Fig. 4). Other bronchioles become dilated or enlarged. The mucus stagnates and bacteria grow. How can we paint this picture vividly? It's like plugged plumbing! (Fig. 5) So far, we've only discussed your mucus-producing cells. What about your army, the ciliated cells?

and the ability to "snap back" like a stretched rubber band when distended by air. This is called *elastic recoil.*

The lungs and bronchial tubes are like a tree surrounded by the chest wall, composed of bone and muscle, which functions like a bellows. The muscles contract and in doing so increase the size of the chest cavity. When the muscles relax, the chest cavity returns to normal. The principal muscles of inspiration, or breathing in, are the diaphragm and the muscles linking the ribs one to the other. When contracting, the diaphragm shortens and pushes downward. At the same time, contraction of the rib muscles raises the rib cage, and in this way the volume of the chest increases during inspiration, or breathing in. The lung is elastic, and so it passively increases in size to fill this newly made space within the chest. As the lung, including the alveoli, enlarges, air from our environment flows in to fill this space. During exhalation, or breathing out, the muscles relax, the elasticity of the lung returns it to a normal size, and air is pushed out, back into the environment.

Ventilation is the term used to refer to the transport of air from the mouth through the bronchial tree to the alveoli and back through the nose or mouth to the outside air. Ventilation, as you can see, equals inspiration and expiration combined. Air is 80 percent nitrogen and 20 percent oxygen; oxygen is vital for the metabolism of our cells and the conversion of foodstuffs into energy. A by-product of this metabolism is carbon dioxide.

Air must pass through the bronchial tree to the alveoli before oxygen can get *into* the bloodstream and carbon dioxide can get *out* because it is the alveoli which are in contact with blood vessels. *Perfusion* refers to the flow of blood through the lungs. *Diffusion* is the term used to describe the passage of oxygen into the bloodstream from the alveoli and the return of carbon dioxide across the delicate membrane between the blood vessels and the alveoli.

The bronchial tree has two kinds of special lining cells. The first type can secrete mucus as a protection against injury and irritation. The second, present from the largest branch (the trachea) down to the smallest branches (the bronchioles), are covered with fine, hair-

ANATOMY

Upper Respiratory System

Mucus

MUCOUS MEMBRANE

Nose
O_2
CO_2
Pharynx
Trachea
Bronchus
Bronchiole

AIRWAY

CO_2
O_2
ALVEOLUS (air sac)

(**Fig. 1**) Anatomy of the Respiratory System. Note the similarity to an upside-down tree. The trachea is the trunk, the bronchi and bronchioles are the branches, and the alveoli the leaves. Oxygen enters and carbon dioxide exits the bloodstream via the alveoli. The mucous membrane contains mucus-producing and ciliated cells.

like structures called *cilia.* The surface of each of
two hundred cilia. In a normal lung, lining cells
stand like an army at attention (Fig. 2). These cel
smooth muscle cells and elastic and collagen fiber
the direction of the mouth and act as a vital defe
cally removing germs and irritating substances. Th
with fine islands of mucus. The mucus helps to
germs.

Summary. During inspiration, what you breathe
the nose, and the back of the throat and is swep
bronchial tree. Because this is the way air flows
airway. Covering cells lining the bronchial tree, cili
beating with an upward motion in your defense. O
mucus to entrap unwanted particulates as another
nism. From the bronchial tree air passes into the alv
gen then diffuses into the blood perfusing the lungs
vital cell functions. Carbon dioxide diffuses into the a
blood and leaves the body during exhalation.

CHRONIC BRONCHITIS

This is a disease characterized by a daily cough
sputum for at least three months each year for two con
when no other disease is present to account for these
rattling cough or frequent clearing of the throat may h
significance as a productive cough. The diagnosis of chr
tis is made by this history, rather than by any abnormali
a chest X ray or even through a pulmonary function te

As the result of cigarette smoking (or, rarely, other i
mucous cells of the bronchial tree respond by excessive pr
their product (Fig. 3). The first sign of excessive productio
is usually morning cough. As cigarette smoking continu
years, the irritation increases, and coughing continues
the day. The excess mucus provides food for bacteria. No
is added to irritation. Mucus changes from clear to yello

Exposure to cigarette smoke for as little as thirty seconds paralyzes cilia for a minimum of fifteen minutes! Continued exposure to cigarette smoke permanently damages the cilia and their ability to beat and to remove mucus, bacteria, and other irritants. This can occur after as little as one year of smoking. Finally, the ciliated cells fall out, leaving you with bald spots! They are replaced with cells that have no defensive properties. *Your army is defenseless!* (Fig. 3, Fig. 6)

As bacteria, no longer cleared by cilia and happily multiplying in excess mucus, grow, PMNs are called into the area as another line of defense. They produce enzymes—chemical substances—to destroy the bacteria, but these enzymes can also damage or destroy the delicate supporting structures of the cells lining the bronchial tree as well as the membranes of the alveoli. In effect, these now become *killer enzymes.* Unfortunately, they kill the good as well as the bad.

EMPHYSEMA

When the air sacs are exposed to cigarette smoke, they also produce a defensive cell called an *alveolar macrophage* (hereafter referred to as AM) (Figs. 7 and 8). AMs engulf irritants and bacteria and call for more PMNs to come into the lungs. The lung tissue, so delicate, flexible, and so important for the passage of oxygen into the bloodstream, with its network of elastins and collagens, also becomes the target for the enzymes or chemical substances produced by the PMNs and the AMs. There are natural defense systems which inhibit the enzymes released by AMs and PMNs, but it appears that this inhibiting function is impaired in smokers. Rarely, an individual may inherit a deficiency in an enzyme inhibitor. This may result in severe emphysema early in life, especially if that individual also smokes. When the elastin and collagen fibers are destroyed, the lung loses its elastic recoil, like a rubber band that won't snap back.

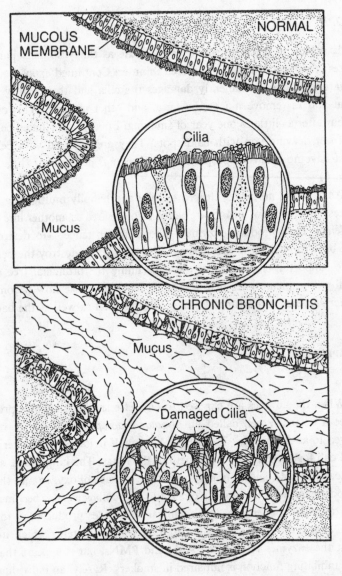

(Fig. 3) Top: Normal Mucous Membrane. Ciliated and mucus-producing cells. Tiny islands of mucus.
Bottom: Chronic Bronchitis. Overproduction of mucus and damaged cells and cilia: the result of cigarette smoking.

and the ability to "snap back" like a stretched rubber band when distended by air. This is called *elastic recoil.*

The lungs and bronchial tubes are like a tree surrounded by the chest wall, composed of bone and muscle, which functions like a bellows. The muscles contract and in doing so increase the size of the chest cavity. When the muscles relax, the chest cavity returns to normal. The principal muscles of inspiration, or breathing in, are the diaphragm and the muscles linking the ribs one to the other. When contracting, the diaphragm shortens and pushes downward. At the same time, contraction of the rib muscles raises the rib cage, and in this way the volume of the chest increases during inspiration, or breathing in. The lung is elastic, and so it passively increases in size to fill this newly made space within the chest. As the lung, including the alveoli, enlarges, air from our environment flows in to fill this space. During exhalation, or breathing out, the muscles relax, the elasticity of the lung returns it to a normal size, and air is pushed out, back into the environment.

Ventilation is the term used to refer to the transport of air from the mouth through the bronchial tree to the alveoli and back through the nose or mouth to the outside air. Ventilation, as you can see, equals inspiration and expiration combined. Air is 80 percent nitrogen and 20 percent oxygen; oxygen is vital for the metabolism of our cells and the conversion of foodstuffs into energy. A by-product of this metabolism is carbon dioxide.

Air must pass through the bronchial tree to the alveoli before oxygen can get *into* the bloodstream and carbon dioxide can get *out* because it is the alveoli which are in contact with blood vessels. *Perfusion* refers to the flow of blood through the lungs. *Diffusion* is the term used to describe the passage of oxygen into the bloodstream from the alveoli and the return of carbon dioxide across the delicate membrane between the blood vessels and the alveoli.

The bronchial tree has two kinds of special lining cells. The first type can secrete mucus as a protection against injury and irritation. The second, present from the largest branch (the trachea) down to the smallest branches (the bronchioles), are covered with fine, hair-

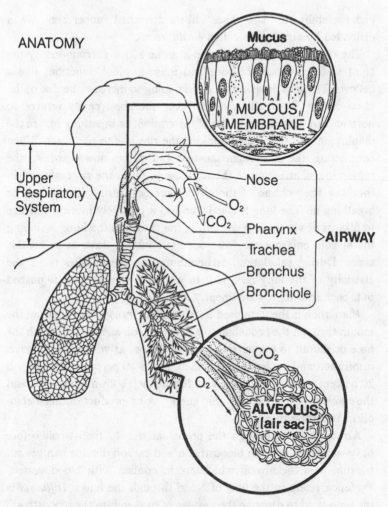

(Fig. 1) Anatomy of the Respiratory System. Note the similarity to an upside-down tree. The trachea is the trunk, the bronchi and bronchioles are the branches, and the alveoli the leaves. Oxygen enters and carbon dioxide exits the bloodstream via the alveoli. The mucous membrane contains mucus-producing and ciliated cells.

like structures called *cilia.* The surface of each of these cells contains two hundred cilia. In a normal lung, lining cells covered with cilia stand like an army at attention (Fig. 2). These cells are supported by smooth muscle cells and elastic and collagen fibers. The cilia wave in the direction of the mouth and act as a vital defense system, physically removing germs and irritating substances. The cilia are covered with fine islands of mucus. The mucus helps to trap irritants and germs.

Summary. During inspiration, what you breathe leaves the mouth, the nose, and the back of the throat and is swept down into the bronchial tree. Because this is the way air flows, it is called the *airway.* Covering cells lining the bronchial tree, cilia, are constantly beating with an upward motion in your defense. Other cells secrete mucus to entrap unwanted particulates as another defense mechanism. From the bronchial tree air passes into the alveoli, where oxygen then diffuses into the blood perfusing the lungs to participate in vital cell functions. Carbon dioxide diffuses into the alveoli from the blood and leaves the body during exhalation.

CHRONIC BRONCHITIS

This is a disease characterized by a daily cough productive of sputum for at least three months each year for two consecutive years when no other disease is present to account for these symptoms. A rattling cough or frequent clearing of the throat may have the same significance as a productive cough. The diagnosis of chronic bronchitis is made by this history, rather than by any abnormalities found on a chest X ray or even through a pulmonary function test.

As the result of cigarette smoking (or, rarely, other irritants), the mucous cells of the bronchial tree respond by excessive production of their product (Fig. 3). The first sign of excessive production of mucus is usually morning cough. As cigarette smoking continues over the years, the irritation increases, and coughing continues throughout the day. The excess mucus provides food for bacteria. Now infection is added to irritation. Mucus changes from clear to yellow since it

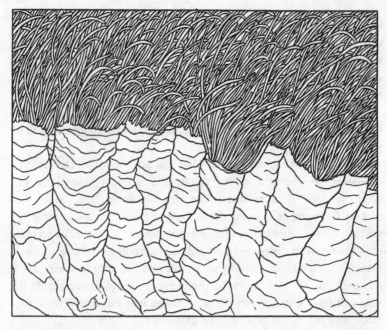

(Fig. 2) Nonsmokers' Army. Ciliated cells lining the airway in a normal lung, standing closely at attention. Artist's rendition adapted from an actual photomicrograph of a lung magnified 4,000. *American Lung Association Bulletin* Vol 64 No 10 (December 1978): 8.

now contains white blood cells (polymorphonuclear leukocytes, hereafter referred to as *PMNs*), defense cells to fight off the infecting organisms by engulfing them. When the bacteria win, the infection becomes deep enough to cause actual destruction of the bronchial wall. Scar tissue replaces the fine cells lining the bronchial tree, and scars give rise to areas of narrowing. Some bronchioles become totally obliterated. *Bronchospasm,* or tightening of the muscles of the bronchial tree, occurs (Fig. 4). Other bronchioles become dilated or enlarged. The mucus stagnates and bacteria grow. How can we paint this picture vividly? It's like plugged plumbing! (Fig. 5) So far, we've only discussed your mucus-producing cells. What about your army, the ciliated cells?

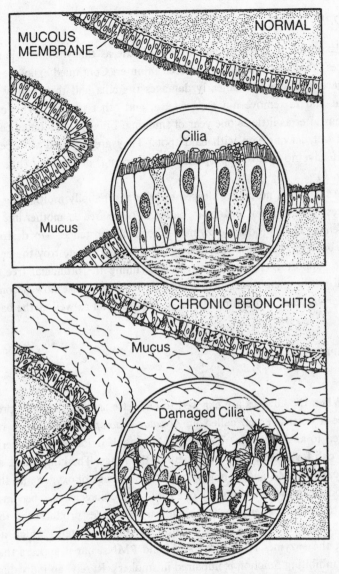

(Fig. 3) Top: Normal Mucous Membrane. Ciliated and mucus-producing cells. Tiny islands of mucus.
Bottom: Chronic Bronchitis. Overproduction of mucus and damaged cells and cilia: the result of cigarette smoking.

Exposure to cigarette smoke for as little as thirty seconds paralyzes cilia for a minimum of fifteen minutes! Continued exposure to cigarette smoke permanently damages the cilia and their ability to beat and to remove mucus, bacteria, and other irritants. This can occur after as little as one year of smoking. Finally, the ciliated cells fall out, leaving you with bald spots! They are replaced with cells that have no defensive properties. *Your army is defenseless!* (Fig. 3, Fig. 6)

As bacteria, no longer cleared by cilia and happily multiplying in excess mucus, grow, PMNs are called into the area as another line of defense. They produce enzymes—chemical substances—to destroy the bacteria, but these enzymes can also damage or destroy the delicate supporting structures of the cells lining the bronchial tree as well as the membranes of the alveoli. In effect, these now become *killer enzymes.* Unfortunately, they kill the good as well as the bad.

EMPHYSEMA

When the air sacs are exposed to cigarette smoke, they also produce a defensive cell called an *alveolar macrophage* (hereafter referred to as AM) (Figs. 7 and 8). AMs engulf irritants and bacteria and call for more PMNs to come into the lungs. The lung tissue, so delicate, flexible, and so important for the passage of oxygen into the bloodstream, with its network of elastins and collagens, also becomes the target for the enzymes or chemical substances produced by the PMNs and the AMs. There are natural defense systems which inhibit the enzymes released by AMs and PMNs, but it appears that this inhibiting function is impaired in smokers. Rarely, an individual may inherit a deficiency in an enzyme inhibitor. This may result in severe emphysema early in life, especially if that individual also smokes. When the elastin and collagen fibers are destroyed, the lung loses its elastic recoil, like a rubber band that won't snap back.

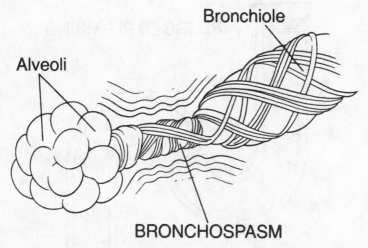

Bronchiole

Alveoli

BRONCHOSPASM

(**Fig. 4**) Bronchospasm. Tightening of the muscles of the bronchial tree, causing narrowing and obstructing the flow of air.

WHEN EMPHYSEMA AND CHRONIC BRONCHITIS MEET

Here's where emphysema and chronic bronchitis get together. After reading this you'll readily see why these two diseases have been lumped under the name chronic obstructive pulmonary disease. As described above, the bronchi are weakened and narrowed by chronic bronchitis. During inspiration, as we told you, respiratory muscles actively contract and keep the airways open. During expiration, when the muscles relax, the air flows rapidly and the pressure in the bronchial tree drops below that of the surrounding lung. The lungs, partially destroyed, are no longer able to put traction on the bronchi to keep them open. Weakened bronchial walls then collapse, choking off the vital flow of air. This is called airway collapse and air trapping (Fig. 9). Weakened by enzymes, the walls of the alveoli rupture and blood vessels die and lung tissue is replaced with scar tissue, leaving areas of destroyed alveoli like "sinkholes," the smaller ones called *blebs* and the larger ones called *bullae* (Fig. 10). The end result is a

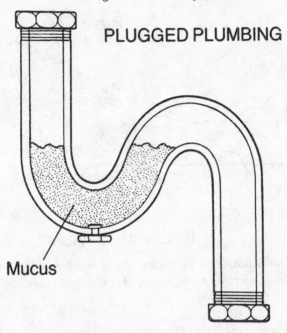

PLUGGED PLUMBING

Mucus

(Fig. 5) Plugged Plumbing. Mucus can totally occlude portions of the bronchial tree.

set of big, overexpanded lungs with a weakened, partially plugged bronchial tree subject to airway collapse and air trapping with blebs and bullae, and breathing, particularly exhalation, becomes a slow, difficult process (Fig. 11). Do you have a big "barrel chest"? Now you know why.

Can anything else go wrong? Absolutely. Next comes mismatched mates. Just as each branch of a tree ultimately leads to a leaf, so in the normal lung each final branch of the bronchial tree leads to an alveolus which is surrounded by blood vessels. In the lung with COPD some of the branches of the bronchial tree become partially or totally blocked by mucus. Blood can easily get to the alveolus but air cannot. The blood leaves the alveolus and returns to the heart and the rest of the body without oxygen.

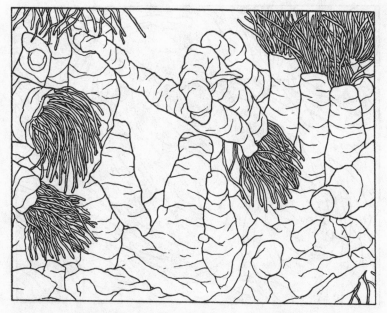

(Fig. 6) The Smoker's Defenseless Army. The cells in the upper right-hand corner are relatively normal. The other cells are falling over and disintegrating. Adapted from an actual photomicrograph of a lung magnified 3000. *American Lung Association Bulletin* Vol 64 No 10 (December 1978): 9.

In other areas of the lung, the bronchial tree may have escaped excessive mucus and be able to transport air. However, the tiny air sacs are now ruptured and the number of blood vessels is greatly reduced. Therefore, when air arrives in the alveolus, there are no blood vessels there to transport their vital cargo to the cells. In other areas of the bronchial tree, alveolar walls and the blood vessels may be totally obliterated. The scientific world calls mismatched mating *ventilation to perfusion imbalance* (Fig. 12).

These mismatched mates, coupled with collapsed airways and plugged plumbing attacked by killer enzymes and defended by a paralyzed army, all paint the picture of COPD. To varying degrees,

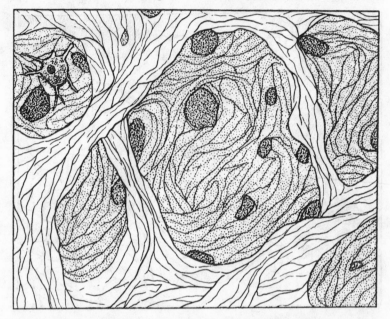

(Fig. 7) Normal Alveoli. There is a macrophage in the upper left-hand corner. The dark areas are pores in the alveolar walls. Artist's rendition. Adapted from an actual photomicrograph of a mouse lung magnified 4000. *American Lung Association Bulletin* Vol 64 No 10 (December 1978): 6.

the person with COPD has a tree with a narrow, defective trunk and sparse leaves.

Is this your story? Or, as physicians call it, your "history"?

You were probably well as a child, with no evidence of respiratory problems. You started smoking in your early teens. After a few years you noticed you had more colds than your nonsmoking friends. After about ten years of smoking, every time you got a cold or upper respiratory infection (URI), it went into your chest. At first, these chest colds would last about two weeks, then about four to six weeks (cilia impaired, mucous glands overproducing in response to irrita-

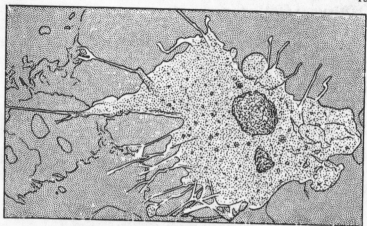

(**Fig. 8**) Alveolar Macrophage. These cells can change their shape remarkably and send out footlike projections which engulf bacteria and irritating particles. Artist's rendition adapted from an actual photomicrograph. *American Lung Association Bulletin* Vol 64 No 10 (December 1978): 6.

tion). Finally, you were left with a morning cough every day which you called a cigarette cough (cilia impaired and ciliated cells beginning to fall out, glands overproducing). Your cough went from morning cough to the ability to bring up sputum any time of the day. Respiratory infections became more frequent and lasted longer. You began to notice that you tired easily, that some tasks were no longer pleasurable. You began to be short of breath when hurrying up a hill or walking up a few flights of stairs (cilia impaired, ciliated cells missing, overproduction of mucus, plugging of bronchial tree, air trapping). Then any type of hurrying frequently began to produce a choking feeling, as though your wind was being cut off (cilia impaired, ciliated cells missing, overproduction of mucus, plugging of bronchial tree, air trapping, airway collapse). With acute infections you began to wheeze or to have bronchospasm in which the air was extremely difficult to get out. Finally, it became difficult to hurry, even on the level. It became difficult to get a day's work done, to

Airway Collapse

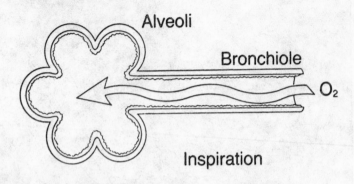

Alveoli

Bronchiole

O_2

Inspiration

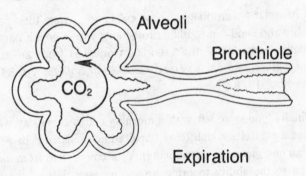

Alveoli

Bronchiole

CO_2

Expiration

(Fig. 9) Airway Collapse and Air Trapping.
Inspiration: Respiratory muscles actively contract to keep the airways open.
Expiration: Damaged lung tissue is no longer capable of holding weakened bronchial walls open, and they collapse and trap air.

perform sex, to do shopping, cooking, cleaning, walking, to care for yourself—and no amount of deep or hard breathing seemed to make any difference (cilia impaired, ciliated cells missing, overproduction of mucus, plugging of bronchi, air trapping, airway collapse, loss of elastic recoil, ruptured alveoli [blebs and perhaps bullae], mismatched mating). Periods of breathlessness increased in intensity,

SINKHOLE

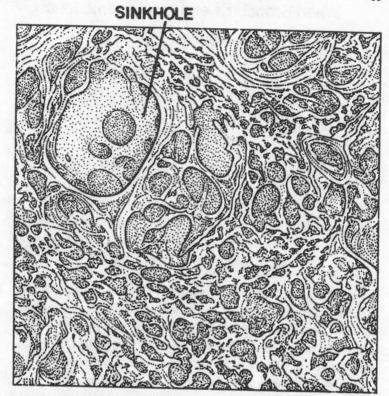

(Fig. 10) A Sinkhole. Destruction of alveolar walls results in large functionless "sinkholes" termed bullae. Artist's rendition of an actual photomicrograph of a lung. *American Lung Association Bulletin* Vol 64 No 10 (December 1978): 5.

especially associated with acute infections (e.g., viruses, pneumonia) or exposure to irritants (air pollutants, smoke), high humidity, or cold air. At these times you may have experienced confusion, insomnia, restlessness, headaches, either a fast, slow, or irregular heart rate, marked shortness of breath, and/or rapid breathing. Intensive therapy may have been necessary, often in a hospital. If you were unable to compensate with usual treatments, then you may have needed artificial ventilation.

When Bronchitis and Emphysema Meet

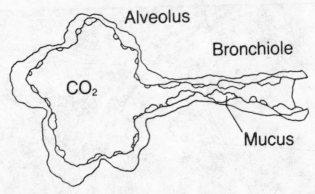

(Fig. 11) When Chronic Bronchitis and Emphysema Meet. The end result is big, overexpanded lungs with a weakened, partially plugged bronchial tree, airway collapse, air trapping, and bullae.

Perhaps this is only part of your story. Perhaps you've already suffered bouts of respiratory failure and had to be on a ventilator. Perhaps you've had pneumonia or recurrent episodes of wheezing (sometimes called *asthmatic bronchitis*) with intermittent increase in obstruction to air flow by plugged airways (called *relapses*). Are you wondering whether you have chronic bronchitis *or* emphysema? Chances are far and away you have both to varying degrees—and either can be serious.

WHERE ASTHMA FITS IN

Asthma is a disease of intermittent airway obstruction characterized by bouts of wheezing due to spasm of the muscles of the airways, and excessive mucus secretion resulting in secondary plugging of the bronchial tree. Unfortunately, in the asthma of adults the exact cause is very seldom known but may be brought on by a variety of things ranging from being upset, or getting a virus or some other respiratory infection, to changes in the barometric pressure or tem-

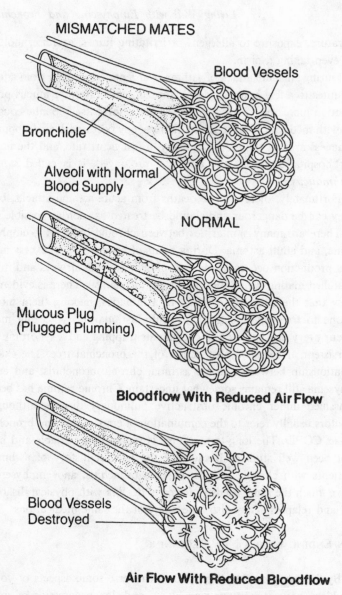

MISMATCHED MATES

Blood Vessels

Bronchiole

Alveoli with Normal
Blood Supply

NORMAL

Mucous Plug
(Plugged Plumbing)

Bloodflow With Reduced Air Flow

Blood Vessels
Destroyed

Air Flow With Reduced Bloodflow

(Fig. 12)

perature, exposure to allergens or irritating fumes, exercise, molds, or even taking aspirin.

During an acute attack of asthma over a period ranging from a few minutes to a few hours or days, wheezing and excessive mucus production increases. If the attack does not resolve itself spontaneously or with medication, then severe distress may occur with air trapping, blueness around the mouth, anxiety, a fast heart rate, and the need for hospitalization. If the attack is prolonged, it is called *status asthmaticus.*

Fortunately, there are few deaths from acute asthma attacks, but they can be dangerous and should be treated as soon as possible.

There are many similarities between chronic bronchitis, emphysema, and adult asthma. During bouts of bronchospasm excess mucus production occurs, leading to plugging of the airways and mismatched mating (ventilation perfusion inequality). There is evidence now that the cilia are impaired in asthmatics, making them more prone to frequent infection. In adults asthma and wheezing may occur every day and lead to chronic air trapping and a syndrome of persistent, irreversible obstruction of the bronchial tree. The exact relationship between chronic asthma, chronic bronchitis, and emphysema still remains somewhat uncertain. Chronic asthma has been classified under chronic obstructive pulmonary disease, although doctors usually refer to the combination of emphysema and bronchitis as COPD. The long-term course is much more variable and has not been well studied. Because of the natural history of asthma, patients with chronic asthma, chronic bronchitis, and emphysema have much the same needs in terms of dealing with physical disability and relapses. They also take many of the same medications.

AN ENDING WITH A NEW BEGINNING

By following our strategy, you can reverse some aspects of your problem, prevent many new problems, and slow progression of your illness. Some things cannot be changed. We cannot repair the sinkholes in your lungs or get you new cilia or strong bronchial walls; we *can* increase your overall respiratory muscle strength and improve the efficiency of your heart and lungs. You'll always be more prone to infections than the next person, but we *can* show you how to protect yourself from *becoming* infected and how to keep the side effects of a relapse or an attack to a minimum. We cannot promise you a life free from medicines and supplemental oxygen, but we *can* teach you how to use your medication and oxygen effectively to minimize the side effects and maximize the benefits.

Your figure may not become that of a bathing beauty or Mr. America; we *can* try to help you to increase your muscle mass, which translates into increased strength, and to normalize your fat content.

We cannot promise you will never land in the hospital; but if admitted, you should be well informed and capable of cooperating. Your knowledge should lessen fears and hasten recovery.

We cannot fashion you into a superathlete or keep you at fever pitch all day. We *can* show you how to be athletic and at the same time conserve energy and do all the tasks you need to do and have energy left over for those you *want* to do.

This book will also discuss having fun, eating well, enjoying sex, working (or working longer), and elevating your mood.

This book is meant to supplement and not to substitute for a good physician, but a knowledgeable patient who takes care of himself may well need fewer visits to the doctor. The patient who tries hard to do right by himself is a pleasure for any physician. With increased comprehension comes appreciation—you and your doctor should both think more of each other. Your functional capacity can improve. We can prove to you that you are a whole, precious person able to take control of your life—and a full one at that. We cannot cure your disease, but we *can* help to arrest or stabilize it.

It's time to get back some of what you've given up, and perhaps find new worlds you never dreamed of. It's time to make your move, *now,* before you have to give up even more. One thing is certain: The old way didn't work. That's why you're reading this book. Try this new way.

2

Smoking and Life Expectancy

AN ASSASSIN EXPOSED

Make no mistake about it, if you smoke, cigarettes are killing you. The U.S. Surgeon General reports that cigarette smoking is the "single greatest preventable cause of death and disability in the United States today." Smoking is the major cause of chronic bronchitis and emphysema. Fifty thousand people will die yearly of these two diseases. If what we told you in Chapter 1 about COPD and smoking interested you but didn't convince you, read on.

Cigarette smokers have approximately double the death rate from heart disease of nonsmokers. Recent evidence suggests that smoking adversely affects the concentration of the "good" cholesterol (see Chap. 4, "Body Business"), decreasing its production. About 1 in 500 cigarette smokers dies from lung cancer each year. This translates to 120,000 people in the United States in 1984. Twenty-two thousand will die from other cancers and 225,000 will die from heart attacks and stroke. If you started smoking at fifteen and smoked the rest of your life, you have half the chance of living to the age of seventy-five as compared with your friend who never smoked.

Don't try to tell yourself that when you smoke, you feel better. You only *think* you smoke to feel good. There is every evidence to suggest that you are seriously dependent. In between cigarettes your nicotine level drops and you feel better when you bring the level back up. No person who coughs up sputum all day, suffers from shortness of breath, easy fatigability, and decreased enjoyment from life smokes for the fun of it. You smoke because you can't help it. What else could that mean but addiction?

The original report of the Surgeon General's Advisory Committee in 1964 stated that smoking had an adverse effect on health, but also alleged that smoking did not fulfill the criteria for addiction for the following reasons: (1) no tolerance developed; (2) there were no withdrawal symptoms; (3) antisocial behavior was not elicited when cigarettes were not available. Now we know better! In 1977 the Royal College of Physicians in London in its report "Smoking and Health" described the nicotine withdrawal syndrome in which there is intense craving, anxiety, irritability, restlessness, depression, inability to sleep, changes in the gastrointestinal system including constipation, and impaired performance when doing such tasks as driving.

As for tolerance, we now know it develops rapidly. By the time you are finished with one pack of cigarettes, you have two hundred jolts of nicotine. This happened with the first pack you ever smoked. At first, perhaps, you were sick when you smoked. You felt dizzy, your heart beat fast, or you were nauseated. Of course, this all went away very rapidly. You began smoking more to get a sense of well-being; you told yourself cigarettes made you less irritable. It was insufficient nicotine, for which you have developed a tolerance, which made you irritable. This is what was relieved by a cigarette. Feeding your addiction makes you feel good.

Violent outbursts have occurred in public places when smokers have been denied access to cigarettes. There it is—antisocial behavior, the last criterion for addiction!

Have you any idea of the effects of smoking on those around you? Researchers recently found actual damage in the airways of children from hundreds of families who had smoking parents as compared with children whose parents did not smoke. Nonsmokers who are exposed to cigarette smoke at work might have the same defects as those people who smoke ten cigarettes a day.

A SMOKER'S RISK/BENEFIT RATIO

Take a piece of paper and in the left-hand column write down all the benefits you receive from smoking. Here are the risks for the right-hand column:

Chronic obstructive pulmonary disease
Heart attack
Cancer of the lung
Cancer of the throat and esophagus
Stroke
Long-term disability as a respiratory or cardiac cripple
Injuring others by direct contact with your cigarette smoke

Is smoking worth it? How many thousands of dollars have you spent on cigarettes? Don't forget to add in the bills for your medical care. Each time you want to smoke a cigarette, think of that risk/benefit ratio. You can *live well* and have a full life. There is only one way to treat smoking—*stop!*

A ONE-SECOND TEST TO DETERMINE YOUR LIFE EXPECTANCY

A one-second test to determine your life expectancy is the forced expiratory volume at one second, known for short as the FEV_1, done after inhaling a bronchodilator. Let us explain this simple test to you. The vital capacity, or VC, is defined as the maximum amount of air which can be exhaled after maximal inspiration. Ordinarily, this test is done on a recording device which not only measures the volume of air but the speed at which it is exhaled. The portion of the vital capacity exhaled in one second is known as the FEV_1. If you inhale a bronchodilator prior to doing the vital capacity, then the FEV_1 after bronchodilators is thus defined. The vital capacity itself, a simple test available in most physicians' offices, is predicted by height and age. The normal FEV₁ is 75% or more of the total normal vital capacity.

This test determines life expectancy *based on your present condition.* No attempt to predict the outcome in any single person can be made because there is much room for change—for better or worse. We have summarized some test results in a simple graph and we ask you to look at where you *might* stand now. (See Table 1.)

Here is how to understand the graph. Take the results of your postbronchodilator FEV₁ and determine into which of the four lines labeled percent predicted FEV₁ it fits. You can then plot the percent of survival at two, five, ten, and fifteen years. For instance, approximately 55 percent of those who have an FEV₁ of 50 percent of predicted are alive at ten years.

A FORMULA TO CHANGE RESULTS OF THE ONE-SECOND TEST

A simple formula to help you change the results of the one-second test: $SS + PD + E = ILE$. Does that sound more complicated than Einstein's $E = mc^2$? The formula stands for Stop Smoking + Proper Diet + Exercise = Increased Life Expectancy. You will learn all the latest information on diet, exercise, and self-care in this book.

This book, however, *cannot* stop smoking for you. After plowing through loads of literature and miracle methods to help people withdraw from cigarettes, we've come to the conclusion that the single best way to stop smoking is to quit cold turkey. You'll have to resign yourself to it—you're going to go through the nicotine withdrawal syndrome.

CALLING IT QUITS—HERE'S HOW

Basically, there are two ways to stop smoking: tapering and quitting. Try quitting first. If you use the alternate route of tapering, make a schedule for yourself. Remember, you are trying to cut down on your nicotine intake each day. You will have a natural tendency to hold the smoke in your lungs longer than before and to smoke the

Table 1   Relationship of Survival to Percent of Predicted Post
Bronchodilator Forced Expiratory Volume at 1 Second (FEV₁)

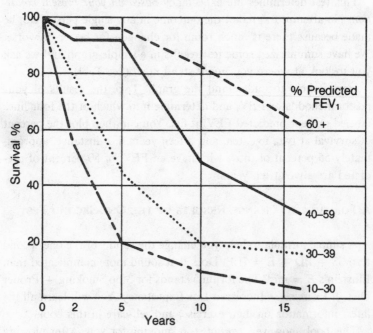

cigarette down to a shorter butt. If you cut down on the tar and
nicotine in your cigarettes or on the number of cigarettes smoked, be
knowledgeable about this fact and don't fool yourself. Remember,
even if you choose to taper, you still must stop completely someday.

You have to have the will, then make the decision, and use some
simple tools. Try chewing gum, nibbling on carrots, having a friend
or mate provide a pleasing alternate sensation, such as a back rub
when the going gets tough. Read books about quitting smoking and
invent some of your own simple tools.

Here is some advice from a pamphlet from the National Cancer
Institute entitled *Clearing the Air:*

Before Quitting:

1. Have a friend quit with you.

2. Switch to a brand which you find distasteful.

3. Smoke only half of each cigarette, and postpone lighting your first cigarette of the day by one hour each day.

4. Decide which hours—odd or even—of the day in which you will smoke.

5. Buy only one pack of cigarettes at a time.

6. Don't smoke under pleasurable circumstances. If you like to smoke in company, only smoke when you are alone.

7. Try to break the "automatic" habit by smoking at odd times of the day and using a different hand to hold your cigarette.

8. Frequent places where smoking is prohibited, such as libraries.

9. Set the date, and then *quit!*

Immediately After Quitting:

1. Continue to visit places where smoking is prohibited.

2. If you miss the sensation of cigarettes, munch on raw carrot sticks or hold a pencil in your hand to fiddle with.

3. Avoid all situations that you associate with smoking, such as watching television or sitting in a special place.

4. Talk to people who don't smoke and avoid your smoking friends for now.

5. Try to change your daily routine.

6. Note your progress on a calendar, especially for the first three months.

7. Drinking large quantities of water and fruit juices may be of help.

Make a regular daily schedule for yourself which does not include cigarettes, and *stick to it!*

Now you've got the will and the tools. Here's something to help you make the decision: signing a personal contract in front of five witnesses.

I, _____, attest that on _____ I will com-
          full name   date
pletely stop smoking. I realize that I am addicted to nicotine and I expect to go through an uncomfortable withdrawal period of several days. During that time I may suffer from intense craving, fearfulness, irritability, restlessness, feelings of sadness, insomnia, constipation, and impaired performance during tasks. During the next week I promise to avoid all people and places that are even remotely connected with cigarette smoking.

I take this pledge and sign this contract as a service to myself as well as to others.

Witnesses:

_____   _____
                                                         signature
_____

_____

_____

3

The Treatment

HELPING YOUR DOCTOR MANAGE YOUR CASE

We hope after reading the first chapter of this book you realize that COPD is characterized by ups and downs and frequent relapses. You should aim to minimize relapses on the one hand and improve your daily functioning on the other. Unchecked relapses result in bouts of severe bronchitis, pneumonia, respiratory failure, hospitalization, and increasing disability and loss of function.

Your doctor is not with you on a daily basis. *You* have to be the one to know when you are beginning a relapse. Based on a sound knowledge of your disease, the doctor will be delighted to hear that you want to be a member of your own health care team. It's important that you have a frank talk with your doctor and explain your new position. Tell him first off you have a better understanding of the disease process.

We hope you're going to tell him that you've stopped smoking (if, of course, you were a smoker), and that you intend to embark on a daily regimen of self-improvement, physical examination, good eating habits, exercise, and healthy thoughts and contacts.

You may be sure the doctor wants a knowledgeable partner helping to handle your case. He wants you to know what you are doing;

know all the names of your medications, their side effects, and perhaps how to manipulate them yourself in certain specific instances; and when to call him early in a relapse. He would rather treat you at the beginning of an infection than see you lying blue in extremis in a hospital bed. Explain that you want to be an effective partner, and that you hope you'll be calling him less but he'll be liking it more. You'll know when to call him and your conversations with him will be intelligent, well-informed, and right to the point. You'll be using his time more effectively. Communicate your urgent desire to get his help in your new program to help yourself. To help you impress him and to provide a review, here's a glossary of terms.

Air trapping: the air caught behind collapsed bronchial branches during expiration (exhalation)

Airway collapse: the actual collapse or closure of branches of the bronchial tree due to weakening of the bronchial walls secondary to disease

Air sacs: delicate sacs at the end of each terminal bronchiole covered with blood vessels, also called *alveoli*

Alveolar macrophage: a special cell in the lung which engulfs bacteria and foreign material and produces enzymes

Alveoli: synonym for air sacs

Asthma: an obstructive disease of the lung which is characterized by bronchospasm and which may be reversible

Asthmatic bronchitis: the coexistence of wheezing and chronic bronchitis

Barrel chest: the shape of the chest in some patients with COPD caused by air trapping which leads to overinflated lungs

Blebs and *bullae* (sinkholes): large holes in the lung due to rupture of the air sacs (alveoli)

Bronchi: branches of the bronchial tree

Bronchial tree: a term used to describe the ductwork of the respiratory system (bronchi and bronchioles) which branch like a tree; the terminal branches lead to the alveoli

Bronchioles: the smallest branches of the bronchial tree; these eventually lead into alveoli or air sacs

Bronchospasm: intermittent narrowing of the bronchial tree because of spasm of the muscles in the bronchial wall

Carbon dioxide: the gaseous waste product secreted by the cells which passes into the air sacs and must exit by way of the bronchial tree

Chronic asthma: a chronic obstructive pulmonary disease which is characterized by bronchospasm and which is not completely reversible

Chronic bronchitis: a chronic obstructive pulmonary disease characterized by cough, chronic infection, and obstruction to the bronchial tree

Chronic obstructive pulmonary disease: a term used to describe a group of diseases characterized by obstruction and destruction of the bronchial tree and/or the alveoli, usually referring to chronic bronchitis, emphysema and chronic asthma

Cilia: tiny hairlike structures on cells lining the bronchial tree which act as a defense mechanism by moving mucus and inhaled particles toward the mouth

Diffusion: the movement of oxygen or carbon dioxide across the delicate membrane of the air sac (alveolus)

Elastic recoil: the ability of the lung to "snap back" at the end of inspiration

Emphysema: a chronic obstructive pulmonary disease characterized by destruction of the alveoli, leading to enlarged air spaces, decreased elastic recoil, and air trapping

Expiration: breathing out

FEV_1 (forced expiratory volume at one second): the amount of air expired in one second during the test of vital capacity

Mucus: a gelatinous product secreted by special cells within the bronchial tree

Oxygen: the most important component of air, necessary for bodily functions

Perfusion: the passage of blood through the lungs

Pharynx: the back of the throat

Polymorphonuclear leukocytes (PMNs): white blood cells—special cells which fight infection, engulf bacteria and irritants, and secrete enzymes

Relapse: getting sick again after feeling well

Trachea: the trunk of the bronchial tree

Ventilation: the passage of air into and out of the lungs

Ventilation perfusion inequality (mismatched mates): the functional deficits which occur when the circulating blood cannot pick up oxygen because of mucus plugs obstructing its flow or when oxygen cannot enter the bloodstream because of destruction of the blood vessels although there is no obstruction to airflow

Vital capacity: the maximum expiration after your deepest inspiration

Wheezing: the sound made by air moving through partially obstructed airways

Look at all you've learned!

To become a top-notch partner, you must learn still more. Study the next section carefully and keep it handy, too, for easy reference. Note that drugs are divided by category according to their uses. Each drug has both a chemical or generic name and a trade or company name. In the chart a trade name is always enclosed in parentheses. In the text a trade name is always capitalized, while a generic name is not. Please note the key on the last page of the chart.

USE OF SPRAYS AND PRESCRIBED GADGETS

Inhalation therapy equipment such as the updraft nebulizer is usually used to facilitate the delivery of a bronchodilator as deep as possible into the respiratory tract. An updraft nebulizer also can instill mucus-thinning agents, antiinflammatory agents, antiasthmatic drugs, and sometimes antibiotics. This equipment is usually driven by an oilless air compressor and is lightweight and convenient to use. In using an updraft nebulizer, merely breathe slowly and

THE MOST COMMONLY PRESCRIBED MEDICATIONS
AND THEIR PRINCIPAL USES AND SIDE EFFECTS

The information in this chart covers the principal uses and side effects of medications discussed but not every possible use or side effect. Know the principal uses, dosage, and side effects of any other medicines you take.

Drug	Why Used	Dosage	Side Effects	Report to the Doctor Immediately
I. BRONCHODILATORS††				
A. *Xanthines***				
Theophylline (Choledyl, Theolair, Theo-Dur, Quibron, et al.)	relieve bronchospasm, reduce wheezing and shortness of breath, improve function of respiratory muscles.	0.5–0.7 mg/kg of normal body weight per 24 hr.—usually about 500–800 mg/day in divided doses	1. nausea 2. stomach pain 3. vomiting 4. trouble sleeping 5. fast or irregular heartbeat 6. confusion 7. vomiting blood 8. loss of appetite 9. irritability, restlessness	1–3 5–8
B. *Beta-Adrenergic stimulants* 1. Metaproterenol (Alupent) liquid		 0.2–0.3 ml diluted in 2.5 ml saline or water	1. nervousness 2. shaking 3. headache 4. rapid or irregular heartbeat 5. nausea 6. muscle cramps	3, 4, 7, 8

Drug	Why Used	Dosage	Side Effects	Report to the Doctor Immediately
			7. chest pain	
			8. vomiting	
			9. weakness	
tablets		20 mg 3–4 times a day		
metered dose inhaler		2–3 inhalations every 4–6 hr., not more than 12 per day		
2. Terbutaline (Brethine, Bricanyl)				
tablets		2.5–5 mg 3–4 times daily		
3. Isoetharine (Bronkosol)				
liquid		1/2 ml diluted with 3 parts saline or water, 4 times a day or every 4 hr.		

Drug	Why Used	Dosage	Side Effects	Report to the Doctor Immediately
metered dose inhaler		2 breaths 4 times a day or every 4 hr., not more than 12 per 24 hr.		
4. Albuterol (Ventolin††, Proventil)				
tablets		2–4 mg 3–4 times a day		
metered dose inhaler		1–2 inhalations every 4–6 hr., not more than 12 per day		
II. ANTIBIOTICS††				
A. *Tetracyclines*	used to combat bacterial infection			1–3, 5–8
1. (Sumycin, Tetrex,†* others)		250–500 mg every 6 hr.	1. burning in stomach 2. vomiting 3. diarrhea 4. increased sensitivity of skin to sunlight	
2. Doxycycline (Vibramycin)*		100 mg every 12 hr. for one day, then	5. rash 6. itching	

Drug	Why Used	Dosage	Side Effects	Report to the Doctor Immediately
		100 mg daily or 100 mg every 12 hr.	7. nausea 8. sore mouth and tongue	
B. *Penicillins†* 1. Ampicillin		250–500 mg every 6 hr.	1. fever 2. hives 3. itching, rash 4. nausea 5. diarrhea 6. wheezing 7. sore mouth and tongue 8. mild stomach upset	1–7
2. Amoxicillin		250 mg every 8 hr.		
C. *Cephalosporins* 1. (Keflex, Velosef, Anspor)		250–500 mg every 6 hr.	1. nausea, vomiting 2. skin rash, hives 3. severe abdominal pain 4. fever 5. severe or persistent diarrhea 6. weakness 7. itching (rectal or genital)	1–6, 9
2. (Ceclor)		250–500 mg every 8 hr.		

Drug	Why Used	Dosage	Side Effects	Report to the Doctor Immediately
			8. mild diarrhea	
			9. sore tongue and mouth	
D. *Erythromycin*[†] (E.E.S.400, Erythrocin, others)		250–500 mg every 6 hr.	1. fever	1–7, 9
			2. hives	
			3. itching, rash	
			4. nausea and abdominal cramps	
			5. diarrhea	
			6. wheezing	
			7. sore mouth and tongue	
			8. mild stomach upset	
			9. dark urine, pale stools, yellow eyes	
E. *Sulfa Drugs*[†****] Trimethoprim-sulfamethoxazole (Septra, Bactrim, regular or double-strength)		2 tablets every 12 hr. or one double-strength tablet (DS) every 12 hr.	1. paleness	1–11, 13–16
			2. black & blue spots	
			3. bleeding	
			4. redness of skin	
			5. weakness, fever	
			6. itching, rash, hives	

Drug	Why Used	Dosage	Side Effects	Report to the Doctor Immediately
Others			7. peeling skin 8. light sensitivity 9. sore tongue 10. turn yellow 11. severe diarrhea 12. headache 13. joint pains 14. hallucinations 15. insomnia 16. pain when urinating	
III. STEROID HORMONES†† A. *Prednisone, Methylpred-nisolone, Dexamethasone* (Medrol, Decadron, others)	decrease bronchospasm, decrease swelling, decrease inflammation, relieve wheezing in bronchial tree.	variable; as little as possible is used to relieve symptoms, but may vary from 1 to 10 or more tablets per day	1. blurred vision 2. frequent urination 3. increased thirst 4. bone pain 5. black stools 6. abdominal pain 7. new infection 8. mood change 9. swelling of feet 10. nervousness	1–7, 9

Drug	Why Used	Dosage	Side Effects	Report to the Doctor Immediately
			11. restlessness	
			12. weight gain	
			13. insomnia	
			14. muscle weakness	
B. *Beclomethasone* (Vanceril, Beclovent)			1. hoarseness	
			2. sore mouth	
metered dose		8–20 breaths per day		
IV. DIGITALIS AND ALLIED CARDIAC GLYCOSIDES				
A. *Digoxin* (Lanoxin)	to improve the strength of contractions of the heart, treat left heart failure, and treat disturbances of heart rhythm	0.125–0.25 mg daily (may be started with higher dose for a few days)	1. loss of appetite	1–8
			2. abdominal pain	
			3. nausea, vomiting	
			4. very rapid, slow, or uneven pulse	
			5. weakness	
			6. blurred, yellow vision	
			7. diarrhea	
			8. mood changes	
			9. breast swelling	

Drug	Why Used	Dosage	Side Effects	Report to the Doctor Immediately
V. DIURETICS††				
A. *Loop diuretic* (most potent)	to prevent excessive fluid retention		1. loss of hearing	1–6, 9
1. Furosemide***** (Lasix)		20–40 mg 1–2 times a day, but very variable up to 200 mg or more daily	2. skin rash, hives 3. bleeding, bruising 4. yellow eyes, skin 5. irregular or fast heartbeat 6. muscle cramps 7. decreased sexual ability (thiazide diuretic) 8. lightheaded, dizzy 9. unusual weakness	
B. *Thiazide diuretics* (less potent)				
1. Hydrochlorothiazide***** (HydroDIURIL)		25–100 mg a day		
2. Dyazide	combination of thiazide diuretic plus a chemical to prevent loss of potassium	1–2 capsules daily		
3. Aldactazide		1–2 tablets daily		
4. Moduretic		1–2 tablets daily		

Drug	Why Used	Dosage	Side Effects	Report to the Doctor Immediately
VI. MAST CELL INHIBITORS†† Cromolyn Sodium (Intal) liquid	a unique category that inhibits the release of chemicals that cause wheezing and bronchospasm	ampules, 1–4 times a day inhaled from a power-driven nebulizer	1. weakness 2. nosebleed 3. wheezing 4. nasal congestion	3
powder		capsules, 1–4 times a day inhaled through a special device called a Spinhaler®		
VII. EXPECTORANT†† Guaifenesin (Robitussin)	thin secretions	1–12 tablespoons a day		
VIII. PARASYMPATHOLYTICS Ipratropium bromide (Atrovent)	a bronchodilator which inhibits the nerves that cause bronchospasm	not as yet released	not as yet released, but apparently free from many side effects associated with other bronchodilators	

Drug	Why Used	Dosage	Side Effects	Report to the Doctor Immediately

KEY: † Take on an empty stomach with full glass of water; allow 1 hr. before and 2 hr. after meals.

†† Could be manipulated with doctor's permission (see later discussion).

* Do not take milk, dairy products, antacids, vitamin-mineral or iron preparations within 2 hr. of taking this medicine.

** Take with food to avoid nausea.

*** Drink additional glasses of fluid unless otherwise directed.

**** Medicine may result in loss of body potassium. Unless otherwise directed, eat foods high in potassium, e.g., citrus fruits, bananas.

comfortably. Try to prolong inspiration by silently counting "one one-thousand, two one-thousand" at the end of inspiration. It's imperative that you keep your equipment clean. Cleaning and sterilization instructions reproduced by permission of the American College of Chest Physicians are as follows (Table 2):

Table 2—Cleaning and Sterilization of Inhalation Therapy Equipment*

1. Each night, wash manifold, tubing, mouthpiece, nebulizer, etc., in mild detergent, such as Joy, Lux, or Ivory. (Equipment should be scrubbed thoroughly.)

2. Rinse the equipment well, making sure all soap is removed.

3. Soak equipment in vinegar solution containing 2 parts of white distilled vinegar with 3 parts distilled water. Soak for 20 minutes.

4. Rinse after soaking in vinegar solution.

5. Let drain dry on *clean* towel (do not wipe or dry with towel).

6. REMEMBER: All water must be removed from the tubing.

7. After equipment is dry, reassemble, ready for use, or store in plastic bag or dust-free area.

NOTE: The Loma Linda University Medical Center has a protocol for the cleaning of home respiratory therapy equipment which varies from the above statement in the following points:

1. After each use, the manifold, mouthpiece, nebulizer, etc., should be disassembled and rinsed thoroughly in hot running water. The parts should be allowed to air dry on a paper towel.

2. Only the mouthpiece need be washed in mild detergent each night.

3. The disinfecting procedure described in the above statement is performed twice a week rather than nightly.

4. The detachable parts are immersed in a white vinegar solution (1 part vinegar, 2 parts water) and allowed to soak for 30 minutes.

* Statement by the Committee on Therapy, American Thoracic Society. *American Review of Respiratory Diseases* 98: 521–22, 1968. As published in John E. Hodgkin, ed., *Chronic Obstructive Pulmonary Disease: Current Concepts in Diagnosis and Comprehensive Care* (Park Ridge, Ill.: American College of Chest Physicians, 1979), p. 65.

5. Hang tubing over a towel rack or shower rod to drain off excess water while drying.

Hand-held nebulizers—such as the DeVilbiss No. 45—do the same thing, but without a motor. When using a hand-held nebulizer, do the following: Hold the nebulizer in an upright position, and place the tip of it just outside your mouth, or teeth, with the lips open; as you are beginning to breathe in, squeeze the bulb rapidly. Continue to inspire slowly, holding your breath at the end, and count "one one-thousand, two one-thousand" before expiration. Breathe out slowly using pursed lips. To clean the DeVilbiss, take out both corks, wash, allow to dry, and put the corks back in.

The proper use of metered dose inhalers (MDIs) was recently studied by Michael T. Newhouse, M.D., at the Regional Chest Unit, St. Josephs Hospital, Hamilton, Ontario, Canada, and reported in *Bronkoscope* Vol. II, no. 2, p. 6. Metered dose inhalers are the easiest and most efficient gadgets we now have to deliver aerosolized medication. Package instructions regarding assemblage and cleaning are very clear. Read them carefully. It behooves you to know the latest information on how to use them with maximal efficiency. Dr. Newhouse's experiment was interesting. He made specially prepared inhalers containing radioactive material and then had volunteers hold them in various positions, inhaling and exhaling at various rates. Here's what he found: The single most important factor in efficient use of an inhaler is to keep the mouth open. The MDI should be held about one and a half inches from a wide-open mouth. Direct the nebulizer to the back of the mouth. Secondly, one should breathe out quietly just before releasing the dose, and then breathe in as slowly as possible over five to six seconds activating the nebulizer until you have reached the height of inspiration. Thirdly, hold your breath as long as possible for a maximum of up to ten seconds. Breathe out slowly against pursed lips (see page 45).

The Aerochamber (Monaghan Medical Corporation) (Fig. 13) and the InspirEase (Key Pharmaceuticals, Inc.) are attachments to most MDIs. Read the package instructions. These devices (called spacers) allow improved delivery of the medication by eliminating the necessity of synchronizing the discharge of aerosol with inspiration. For use of the inspiratory muscle trainer, please see Chapter 5, "Exercise."

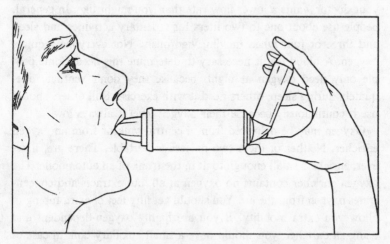

(**Fig. 13**) Aerochamber Aerosol inhaler. The Aerochamber is a cylinder which attaches to the mouthpiece of any MDI and allows efficient inhalation of the spray without the necessity of synchronizing the discharge of medication with inspiration.

New gadgets will be coming out, and there are some we may have missed. Make sure that a knowledgeable person such as a respiratory therapist, your doctor, or his assistant shows you how to use each device correctly; and know exactly how to keep it clean and troubleshoot any minor problems.

As with any other medication, know exactly how much and how often when it comes to things you inhale.

OTHER IMPORTANT THERAPIES

Supplemental Oxygen. This is a wonderful drug and may be essential to your functioning. Some people worry about becoming ad-

dicted to oxygen. That can't happen. It is possible, however, for you
to be extremely oxygen-sensitive and that too much oxygen may
actually suppress your respirations. This will not happen if you follow your doctor's instructions. You should know about that in case
your doctor wants a lower flow rate than you might like. In general,
people use about one to two liters for sedentary activities and sleep
and three or four when moving vigorously. Not everyone requires
oxygen. A blood test is necessary to determine this need. Some people only need oxygen at night, because they don't ventilate adequately during sleep; others need it with exercise. Still others should
use it continuously because their oxygen level is always low.

Oxygen may be delivered from a central tank or from an oxygen
enricher. Neither of these two devices is portable. There are, however, enrichers small enough to fit in the trunk of an automobile. The
oxygen enricher contains no oxygen at all, but extracts and concen-
trates oxygen from the air. You should get fifty feet of extra tubing to
allow you extra mobility. If you are highly oxygen-dependent and
using an enricher, you should have a small auxiliary tank in case of
an electrical power failure.

In general, for people who desire mobility, we recommend the
liquid oxygen system with a central tank and a portable auxiliary
container, either with an over-the-shoulder strap (Fig. 14) or with a
stroller, like a luggage carrier. The auxiliary tank contains up to
eight hours of oxygen, depending on the liter flow you require.

When using oxygen, you should never be within five (5) feet of a
flame. Oxygen is *not* flammable but will greatly enhance the combus-
tion of other substances. Follow the advice of your oxygen supplier.

Oxygen decreases the work of breathing and lessens the strain on
your heart. It corrects a lack of blood oxygen which can otherwise
occur when you don't breathe as deeply during sleep as you do during your waking hours. In addition, oxygen improves your ability to
exercise, and more exercise means better muscle mass and more
strength. The ability to exercise means a lot of other things, too.
You'll read more about that in our special chapter covering the subject. Studies have shown that, when needed, the use of oxygen pro-

longs life, and the more continuous the therapy the better the survival. As stated above, all patients with COPD, however, do not require supplementary oxygen. Your doctor is the best one to know whether you do or do not.

If you do require oxygen, make sure you know the exact liter flow required for sleep, sedentary activities, activities of daily living (including toileting), sex, and exercise.

Pursed-Lip Breathing. Pursed-lip breathing is a useful tool to keep your airways open. Breathe in through the nose and on expiration, purse your lips, taking twice as long to breathe out, as though you were going to whistle. This does not allow the air to flow out of the bronchial tree as rapidly. Keeping the flow rate down keeps the pressure up, and this prevents airway collapse. Use pursed-lip breathing whenever you like, including during exercise. Do it if it makes you feel better, and disregard it if it doesn't.

Postural Drainage. Everything in this world runs better downhill than uphill, and with postural drainage you are trying to get your secretions to run downhill, to facilitate their removal. You should practice postural drainage right after you use your bronchodilator *if it is helpful* and results in increased clearing of secretions. If it does not, postural drainage is not necessary. Here are some simple postural drainage positions done in bed using two or three pillows (Fig. 15). Your doctor may prescribe others.

While you are doing postural drainage, if somebody is with you, cupping or vibration to the back may help to shake the secretions loose. In cupping, the fingers of the hands are held together like a cup and a gentle alternating tapping motion is made over the chest, or, alternatively, there are small, inexpensive back vibrators available. If cupping or vibration makes your ribs sore, desist—or modify so the motions are not as vigorous. Do cupping and vibration only on the rib cage. Avoid the spinal column, breast bone, or breasts. Do postural drainage on an empty stomach.

It is extremely important to get the volume of secretions down to the lowest possible amount every day. The use of bronchodilators, antibiotics, postural drainage, cupping, and vibration all aim to ac-

(**Fig. 14**) Liquid Oxygen. You can take it with you wherever you go.
Keep five feet away from any flame.

complish that end. With secretions out of the way, your passages are
free to transport air. With secretions in the way, they're plugged up,
just as we described in Chapter 1.

(Fig. 15) Postural Drainage. (A) First on your abdomen. (B) Then on each side. Remain in each position for five minutes and follow each position with a therapeutic cough.

Fluids. Fluids, containing water, will help to loosen secretions. Drinking six to eight glasses of water a day is generally acceptable and is thought to help thin out thick sputum. In some cases water restriction is necessary. It will then be prescribed by your doctor. Soda, tea, coffee, milk, and juices are predominantly water.

Effective Coughing. A good therapeutic cough is another key item in clearing secretions. Sit up, your head flexed forward, your shoulders relaxed in a slight forward position, your feet on the floor, a pillow held to your abdomen. Lean forward slowly, blowing out using pursed-lip breathing. Begin to sit up, and as you do so slowly "sniff" the air in, feeling your abdomen push out against the pillow. (Do not take fast breaths at this point. You want to get a nice column of air behind your mucus plugs to help push them out when you actually give your therapeutic cough.) Repeat three or four times, refraining from actually coughing. When you feel ready to cough, take a good, deep breath, pushing the pillow out, then lean forward once again, using gravity to help you. Begin your cough by making a false, stuttering (or staccato) cough, trying to get enough force present to maximize air flow and secretion outflow without causing airway collapse. Keep your mouth open while coughing (but please prevent infection of others by using a handkerchief) (Fig. 16). Do a therapeutic cough after completing each postural drainage position.

SELF-EVALUATION: A THREE-MINUTE DAILY PHYSICAL EXAM

You've learned all about drugs and supplementary therapy. Now it's time to go one step further in the great task of becoming a member of your own health care team. You have to be able to do a good physical examination on yourself for early detection of problems. You want to know exactly how you're doing and when additional therapy or a visit to the doctor might be important. With a little practice, three minutes or less a day will do it. You'll soon become an expert and pick up minor changes in yourself which could be significant long before you might be going to the doctor for your appointment. Here's your daily physical exam explained in detail. We'll follow it with an easy-to-record chart. Do your physical at the same time each day if you can.

1. Take your resting pulse (ideally, you should have been sitting for at least five minutes and not exercising for at least half an hour) for thirty seconds and multiply by two. (For how to take your pulse, see Chap. 5.)

2. Check your respiratory rate for thirty seconds and multiply by two. Respiratory rates vary widely, especially when you are concentrating on them. After doing this every day you'll soon learn the variations which are acceptable for you.

3. Put your hand on the back of your neck and then on your forehead; learn to know when you feel hot. Take your temperature if you are uncertain or not feeling up to par.

4. Test cough, that is, give a resounding cough and listen. Having no sputum is normal. You should know what your baseline cough is; only then can you determine that the volume of your secretions might be increasing. This is a critical part of your daily physical exam, for the increase in the volume of secretions heralds the onset of a relapse. Grade your test cough 0 to 4+.

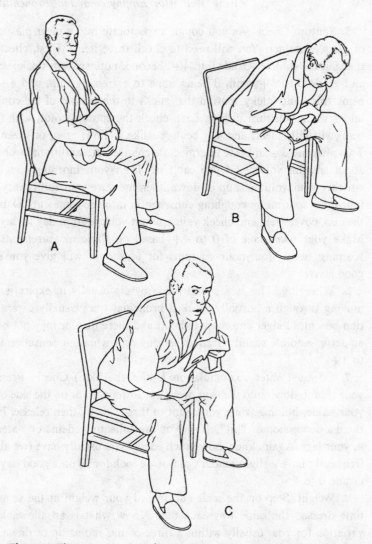

(Fig. 16) Therapeutic Cough: (A) Proper starting position, feet supported, shoulders relaxed, knees flexed. (B) Lean forward slowly, exhaling with pursed-lip breathing. (C) Final cough position, mouth open. See text for complete sequence.

5. Sputum Check. As you cough, expectorate into a clear plastic or glass container. You will need to check three items. First, check the sputum volume. Grade 0 to 4+. Second, note sputum thickness and grade 0 to 4+, with 0 being none to extremely thin, and 4+ being thick and sticky sputum that sticks to the bottom of the container when you turn it over. Last, check the sputum color, with 0 being virtually clear, and 4+ being puslike, yellow, gray, or green. Two plus and 3+ indicate intermediate changes. An additional word about sputum volume. If you can't tell from your morning cough whether your volume is up or down, then measure your full twenty-four-hour sputum by coughing consistently into the same cup. Date the cup, cover well, and check your sputum volume from day to day. Make your own scale of 0 to 4+ based on these measurements. Keeping twenty-four-hour sputums for four days will give you a good start.

6. Wheezing. This is a sound made by air usually in expiration moving through a partially blocked bronchial tree. Usually expiration becomes longer and more difficult and there may or may not be an actual audible sound. Grade wheezing or a wheezing sensation 0 to 4+.

7. Edema (Water Accumulation Under the Skin) Check. Press your thumb down into the skin over your lower shin or on the side of your ankle, holding while you count to three slowly, then release. Is there a depression or "pit"? If so, you are collecting edema or water in your legs. Again, know how much edema you usually have (we all frequently have a slight amount of it if we look for it) on a good day. Grade 0 to 4+.

8. Weight. Step on the scale and record your weight at the same time dressed the same way each day. Know what is an allowable variation for you, usually within a three-pound radius up or down.

9. Functional Capacity. Now walk rather briskly around the room. Stretch, and think about yourself. How do you feel in an overall way? Is your chest tight and constricted? Are you mobilizing or producing secretions easily? Can you walk around the room without undue difficulty? Do you feel calm as opposed to anxious? Do you have air hunger as opposed to what you consider to be "normal" respiration? Look at yourself critically. You will have ups and downs, and you must learn what are minor variations that require no change in your treatment, and what changes in your breathing pattern, respiratory rate, and functional capacity are significant. Call your functional capacity poor, good, or excellent; or perhaps you rate yourself fair. The use of the terms is flexible as long as you know what they mean.

Self-evaluation Diary

Here's a diary to help you record your physical examination. Note that you may have to keep the diary for a whole week to be able to fill in columns 1 and 2, the examination findings on a good day and the usual variation. Also note that once you are used to keeping the diary you may "look back" at information in columns 1 and 2, and in subsequent weeks you only need to record the daily changes.

MANIPULATING YOUR MEDICATIONS (WITH PERMISSION)

You've learned the uses and side effects of all the medicines you take, and you can make an intelligent self-evaluation; now we can go yet a step further. *With your doctor's permission,* you can learn to manipulate certain of your drugs at specific times based on your own physical examination. To do this you need your doctor's absolute cooperation. If he says it isn't right for you, it isn't. You may find, however, that once you indicate your knowledge and willingness to help in your care that he's more than happy to allow you this latitude. Perhaps you already have antibiotics you keep and take whenever the volume of your secretions increases. Here's some of the ways that medications can possibly be manipulated safely and the specific times and the specific symptoms or physical findings you might want to change them for.

1. You might not require full therapeutic doses of bronchodilators on a daily basis; and during attacks of acute wheezing, you may be

SAMPLE SELF-EVALUATION DIARY

Week of _____

	Examination Findings On a Good Day	Usual Variation	Mon	Tue	Wed	Thr	Fri	Sat	Sun
Resting pulse	80	80-95	90						
Resting respiratory rate	20	16-24	18						
Temperature by touch	Normal	-	Norml.						
Test cough 0-4+	1+	0-2+	1+						
Sputum volume 0-4+	1+	1-2+	1+						
Sputum thickness 0-4+	1+	1-2+	2+						
Sputum color 0-4+	1+	1-2+	1+						
Wheezing 0-4+	0	0-1+	0						
Edema 0-4+	0	0	0						
Weight	160	157-160	158						
Functional Capacity: Poor Good Excellent	G	G-E	G						

instructed to increase the number of tablets of your bronchodilator, e.g., Alupent, Ventolin, etc., by one or two tablets a day, risking some nervousness or shakiness.

Another way to maximize bronchodilator effect is to increase the number of inhalations a day from the metered dose inhaler, i.e., increase from two breaths four times a day to two breaths every four hours. You might not be at the maximum number of drops for the bronchodilator you use in the updraft nebulizer, and the frequency of use there might also be increased by your physician from four times a day to every four hours day and night.

2. Whenever the volume of your secretions increases significantly or whenever there is a consistency or color change you definitely associate with a relapse, you might be allowed to take antibiotics, which you keep on hand specifically for that purpose, for seven to ten days.

3. Instructions to avoid a prolonged attack of wheezing may be, for example, to take six extra tablets of prednisone early on and then decrease the daily dose by one tablet every several days thereafter, providing you feel better, until you are back to your maintenance dose.

4. Are you a person who gains water weight? You usually know this by a weight gain of more than three pounds or a noticeable "pit" on self-examination. Doctors frequently allow patients to take an extra one to two tablets of diuretic on those days along with an increase in supplemental potassium. If you do take supplemental potassium now, let's say twenty to forty milliequivalents per day, here's an easy way to tell how much extra to take. Measure all your urine output for twelve to twenty-four hours after taking extra diuretics. For every quart of urine over two quarts (your usual daily output) you might require twenty extra milliequivalents of potassium.

5. Cromolyn sodium (Intal) can be increased before and during your bad seasons if you have allergies. The number of puffs of beclomethasone can also be increased. Cromolyn sodium and

beclomethasone are *not useful* in *acute* attacks of wheezing. They *prevent* future attacks.

6. Expectorants such as guaifenesin can be increased or added to your daily regimen whenever secretions thicken.

7. With an exacerbation of your illness you may require more oxygen. A typical regimen when you have increased difficulty in breathing might be: sleep and sit, one to two liters; eat and slow walking, three to four liters; defecation and activities of daily living, three to four liters.

Now it's time to have a talk with your doctor about this whole business of changing your medication during an acute exacerbation of your illness. For that, we've provided a chart called the Therapeutic Manipulation Chart (Table 3). It's really a detailed patient instruction form and it's purely optional between you and your doctor. Perhaps you already have instructions to change some drugs in case of a relapse or wheeze. The number and names of medications you manipulate may change at any time, depending on what works and what doesn't work for new changes in your condition. Use this chart to work out allowable changes in regimen with your physician. To utilize the chart properly, fill in the names and usual doses of your medications (Col.1). We have completed Column 2 for you. Your doctor can then scan your drug regimen, checking yes or no and filling out the details on the "yes" drugs.

RELAPSE AND PROGRESS—KEEPING TRACK

Shouldn't you let bygones be bygones and put relapses out of mind and concentrate on the good times? In spirit, yes; in documentation, no. You want to pin down exactly what happened before and during a relapse—what was done and what worked (and what didn't). You must be a good detective and share the information you've got stashed away with your physician when the same syndrome happens again.

It's important to follow your progress toward recovery when you have a bad spell. Record events accurately (Table 4). If you need to, keep an allergy record as well.

WHEN TO CALL THE DOCTOR (HE'LL BE GLAD YOU DID)

You know you should call the doctor when you are extremely short of breath, feel very ill, have a high temperature or chest pain, or cough up blood. What we're talking about here is calling the doctor *before* you become this ill, when the signs and symptoms are just beginning. You obviously have to make some choices; you can't call the doctor for every symptom or sign. However, after reading this chapter, you are in a position to make educated decisions. Let's say you have completed your physical exam for the day and note abnormalities which although perhaps not immediately alarming should now alert you to the fact that you may be suffering a relapse. Do you have any instructions on your therapeutic manipulation chart? If so, follow them! Continue to assess your physical examination every few hours throughout the day if necessary.

Are things getting better, or worse? It takes twenty-four to thirty-six hours for sputum to begin to return to normal after an antibiotic is started. Temperature should abate within twenty-four to thirty-six hours. After a diuretic is taken, improvement in edema should occur within a few hours to a day. If your pulse is, for example, ten beats above your normal variation, this may not come down until wheezing and shortness of breath lessen and your cough returns to a more normal thickness, volume, and color. If your pulse remains persistently above its normal variation and you are feeling worse, let your doctor know. The doctor will be glad that you called.

If there is a positive finding on your physical exam which indicates to you that you are on the verge of a significant relapse, or when, having manipulated your medications to the best of your ability, you realize that you are not getting better, your doctor should hear from you.

Perhaps you're not gasping but you know you're not well either, and at the moment it's too complicated for you to figure out whether

SAMPLE THERAPEUTIC MANIPULATION CHART

March 4, 1985

Patient please complete ▶ Doctor please complete ▶

Drugs Name/usual dose, if any	Reasons Why You Might Manipulate the Drug	Suggested Manipulation	No	Yes	(Dr. please elaborate if necessary)
Bronchodilator tablet: theophylline 250 mg 2x/day (fill in name/dose)	Increased wheezing and shortness of breath	___ extra tablets ___ x per day	X		
Bronchodilator spray: albuterol, 2 inhale every 6 hr. (fill in name/dose)	Increased wheezing and shortness of breath	Increase to 2 breaths every 4 hr.		X	while awake until improved and then reduce to usual dose. Stop and notify me if you notice a rapid or irregular heart action.
Bronchodilator drops: (fill in name/dose)	Increased wheezing and shortness of breath	Increase by ___ drop(s) and use every ___ hr.			
Antibiotic: doxycycline, 100 mg (fill in name/dose)	Increase in thickness or volume of sputum; significant color change; fever	1 tablet(s) every 12 hr. x 10 days		X	Call me if no improvement within 36 hours.
Steroid: prednisone, 5 mg 2 x/day (fill in name/dose)	Increased wheezing and shortness of breath	Take 6 tablet(s) x 2 days, then decrease by 1 tablet(s) every 2 days until baseline dose		X	Divided into 2 daily; draw if necessary - otherwise take in one dose before breakfast. Notify me within 12 hours of beginning this regimen.

	Increased edema (water accumulation)	extra tablets daily x ____ days	X	Call me if edema occurs or daily weight increases by 3 pounds.
Diuretic: Furosemide, 40 mg/day (fill in name/dose)				
Expectorant: (fill in name/dose)	Increased thickness of sputum	____ tbsp./tablets ____ x per day x ____ days		
Other:				

This chart is not applicable to any individual. Work out your chart with your Doctor.

Table 4

RELAPSE PROGRESS DIARY
Dates: _3/4/85_ to _3/9/85_

Changing Signs/Symptoms	Measures Taken	What Happened
Resting pulse _120_	1) 3/4/85 postural drainage increased to every 4 hours	3/4/85 chest tight but no severe distress
Respiratory rate _30_	2) steam added	sputum greenish, large volume
Temperature _101_	3) ampicillin, 500mg every 6 hours	3/5/85 volume sputum less, color gray, less tightness
Test cough secretions _3+_	4) increased fluids to 8 glasses per day	P115 R24 T98.6
Sputum volume _3+_		
Sputum thickness _3+_	5) albuterol spray increased to 2 breaths every 4 hours	3/6/85 definitely better - secretions thinner - not so tight, no temp
Sputum color change _2+_		
Wheezing _2+_		P110 R20 T98.6
Edema _0_	6) prednisone, 6 tabs 3/4/85 - then ↓ by 1 every 2 days	3/7/85 almost back to self P100 R16 T98.6
Weight _same_	7) physician called 3/4/85, 3/5/85, 3/6/85, to call back if not back to baseline by 3/10	3/8/85 better P90 R16 T98.6
Functional capacity _poor_		3/9/85 back to baseline P85 R16 T98.6

you should be increasing your diuretics, steroids, bronchodilator, or whatever else is on your instruction sheet. You can still call the doctor and discuss it with him. He'll be glad that you did. Explain your physical findings. Have your medication chart ready and any ideas that you might have as to what usually helps you when you have these physical findings. Your doctor's advice will be much more effective if you, or your spouse, call and can clearly explain the problem: "Doctor, my overall functional capacity appears to be decreased. I have a thick cough, and my sputum has turned a gray-green color. My pulse is up over its usual level by twenty beats a minute, and my respiratory rate is higher by four breaths a minute. I have no fever. My weight is up by four pounds. What do you suggest? Do you think I should take an antibiotic and one extra tablet of my diuretic? Am I sick enough to come in for a visit?"

How can you be *sure* that when you call the doctor he'll be glad you did? Ask him when you should call, and do this well in advance of any possible need for such a call. Show him the physical exam checklist. He might want to add or subtract from it. If, for instance, you always have about $1+$ or $2+$ fluid in your legs, let's say, from chronic venous disease, you may not have to call him or do anything if the swelling in your legs increases a little bit. It's not too hard to know you should call the doctor when you're blue and gasping. Your responsibility—and your doctor can share it with you—is to know when to call him early in a relapse.

SELF-PROTECTION

We think self-protection rightly belongs under therapy. Prevention is the best treatment. Self-protection deserves a major commitment on your part. Here are some of the hazards to know about. Knowing gives you the ability to cope or avoid.

Excessive Heat. Nature dictates that we maintain our body temperature at about 98.6° F. The closer the outside temperature comes to body temperature the harder you must work to maintain a normal body temperature of about 98.6°. If body temperature rises above normal, heart work is increased and dilation of blood vessels in skin occurs to eliminate the excess heat. If it is above 83° outside, no vigorous walking or exercising is advisable unless the humidity is very low. The body maintains normal temperature by evaporation of fluid or sweating; evaporation of sweat cools the body. When the air, however, is filled with water, it is much more difficult, and this process is less efficient. Therefore, before exercising outside, check the temperature and humidity in the following chart (Table 5).

From studying the chart you can see that when the temperature is 75° and the humidity is 60 percent, you are entering the danger zone. If you are like most of our patients with significant COPD, you should definitely not exercise outside. An air conditioner that reduces the surrounding temperature as well as the humidity is important for you. On the other hand, when the temperature is down around 70°, the ideal humidity is between 40 and 60 percent. You should try to keep your home at this temperature the year round. Your secretions will be the loosest and your body will work efficiently.

Excessive cold stresses the body's ability to maintain its normal temperature. The older we get, the more difficult it is for us to keep our temperature at 98.6° when the environment is very cold. In addition, for many patients with COPD, cold air can induce an attack of bronchospasm. Do not go out for any length of time if the temperature is below 25° F. When exposing yourself to cold in the winter, make sure you're wearing a hat pulled down over the ears, since a great deal of circulation goes through the scalp. Use mittens instead of gloves, since one finger can warm the other. To warm inspired air, use a scarf over the face, tucked under the brim of your hat, or a cold-weather face mask, easily obtained at drugstores. Long underwear designed to wick away sweat is advisable since sweating following exertion in a cold atmosphere results in an icelike fluid on your skin and you may become hypothermic. Dress in layers (see Chap. 5, "Exercise").

The windchill factor is announced throughout the day on radio and television and is a measure of the cooling effect of windy conditions. You lose more heat when the wind is blowing than when it is

Table 5

TEMPERATURE AND HUMIDITY

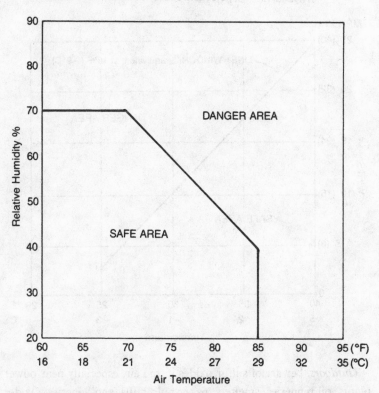

calm. Therefore, the windchill factor expresses the effective temperature for you in terms of the prevailing coldness as well as the speed of the wind. Consult the enclosed Windchill Chart to note when it's either safe or dangerous for prolonged time in the cold (Table 6).

Air Pollution

Smog and air pollution are very dangerous and can result in wheezing, airway injury, loss of precious functional capacity, and sometimes even death.

Table 6

WINDCHILL CHART

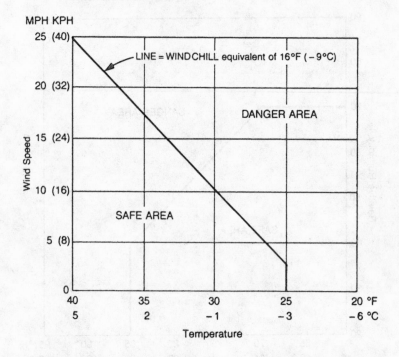

Outdoors, beware of sulfur oxides in the air, especially near power plants, oil refineries, smelters, paper pulp mills, and wineries. Oxides of nitrogen pollute air near power plants and oil refineries and are extruded from automobile exhausts, which also produce ozone. Pollens, which cause hay fever, affect up to 5 to 10 percent of the U.S. population, usually beginning in mid-August; allergies to trees and grasses occur in early spring and allergies to molds occur in the fall. Do not go out in smog. Avoid walking outside in the city when the traffic is extremely heavy. Walk outdoors in the early morning and avoid altogether any dusty outside atmosphere. Check TV and radio for the air quality index. If you have "bad seasons," protect yourself by using pollen masks (available at drugstores), air conditioners, and air filters, and by staying in.

Exposure to grain dust (in the vicinity of grain elevators) and castor bean dust (near castor bean plants) has been known to result in asthma.

Indoors, beware of sulfur oxides emitted in large amounts from kerosene space heaters and oxides of nitrogen emitted from kerosene heaters or stoves and stoves burning natural gas, wood, or coal. Significant in-house allergens may result from animal dander, house dust and house dust mites, chemicals, and sprays.

Air pollution can also cause cancer—e.g., the inhalation of arsenic near sources such as smelters, and polycyclic hydrocarbons which are emitted from diesel engines and petroleum refineries. Arsenic is also present in tobacco smoke and is found in high concentrations indoors, along with radon daughters emitted from construction materials and asbestos from ceiling and floor tiles, sprayed on insulation, and the insulation outside and at times inside boilers and heating ducts. The incidence of lung cancer is higher in families of asbestos workers and among nonsmoking spouses of smokers as opposed to spouses of nonsmokers.

Smoke—and by this we mean other people's smoking—is a hazard you must avoid. If a person sharing a home with you smokes, it's as though you were exposed to a minimum of ten cigarettes a day. Do not stay in the same room with anyone smoking. Put up No Smoking signs in your home and throw out any ashtrays. If friends want to smoke, ask them to step outside your home. If your mate smokes, the same applies. Your atmosphere needs to be smoke-free.

Talcum powder and hairspray can be inhaled into the lungs. If you must use a powder, use cornstarch. Certain commercial body powders are made with cornstarch instead of talc (your druggist can tell you which ones). Forget hairsprays; they may aggravate your breathing difficulty.

Your Occupation. Your job could be adversely affecting your lungs. Repetitive inhalation of any number of various chemicals or substances may produce classic asthma. Failure to recognize occupational asthma may result in permanent disability. Check your occupation against the following:

Industrial Material	Industry	Irritant	Etiology Pharmacological	Allergic
Ammonia, sulfur dioxide, hydrochloric acid, chlorine, nitrogen dioxide	Chemical and petroleum, silo fillers	+		
Urea, formaldehyde	Metal foundries			
Formalin	Medical	?		?
Animal, bird, fish, and insect serum, dander secretions	Veterinarians, animal and poultry breeders, laboratory workers, fishing industry, sericulture			+
Castor bean	Oil and food			+
Green coffee bean				+
Papain				+
Pancreatic extracts				+
Enzymes from *Bacillus subtilis*	Detergent			+
Hog Trypsin	Plastics, rubber, and resin			+
Ethylene diamine				+
Phthalic anhydride				
Trimellitic anhydride				+
Phenylglycine acid chloride	Pharmaceutical			+
Sulphone chloramides				+
Complex salts of platinum	Metal refining		?	+
Salts of nickel	Metal plating			?
Flour	Bakers, farmers, grain elevator operators			?
Grain				?
Wood dusts	Wood mills, carpenters			?
Vegetable gums (acacia, karaya)	Printers			?
Ampicillin	Pharmaceutical			?
Spiramycin				?
Piperazine				?
Amprolium hydrochloride				?

Toluene diisocyanate	Polyurethane	?	?	?
Pyrolysis products of PVC price labels	Meat wrappers	?		?
Soldering fluxes	Electrical trade	?		?
Organic phosphorous insecticides	Farm workers		?	
Cotton dusts	Textile, vegetable oil		?	?

Reprinted permission *Practical Cardiology,* May 15, 1982.

Hobbies can be culprits. The list of arts and crafts materials that can cause lung damage is long. They include the following:

- Solvents found in lacquers and other thinners, paint removers, cleaners and other materials
- Metals such as lead, cadmium, and uranium found in pigments, pottery glazes, solders, photochemicals, and alloys
- Mineral dusts like crystalline silica and asbestos found in stones, clays, and pottery glazes
- Gases such as chloride, nitrogen dioxide, and sulfur dioxide produced as a by-product of welding, photo processing, kiln and foundry firings, and similar processes
- Chemicals such as acids and alkalis used in a variety of arts and crafts processes, including etching, photography, and textile dyeing

Information reproduced from *American Lung Association Bulletin* 69, no. 3 (May/June 1983).

If your hobby is important to you and you need to protect yourself, wear a protective mask. Masks can be purchased from industrial supply and safety firms.

Make sure ventilation is more than adequate when engaging in a hobby with even the slightest potential for lung damage.

Home. You spend at least ten hours a day at home (mostly in the bedroom). You may be sensitive or "allergic" to many more things than you ever realized. Sensitivities or allergies to foreign substances contribute to bronchospasm. You should try to remove sources of dust, mold, feathers, animal dander, and other allergens and irritating substances from the environment. Here are some suggestions.

Use the ones you feel are pertinent for you, and before you pass these suggestions off as unimportant and too much trouble, remember, house dust can be an unexpected culprit in relapses of COPD.

A. Bed

1. Use zippered, allergen-proof covers (usually plastic) on pillows, mattresses, and box springs. Seal zippers with heavy tape.

2. Do not store anything under the bed.

3. Use pillows and blankets made of Dacron or other synthetics rather than down or feathers.

4. Use a short comforter (no feathers) instead of a bedspread (see Chap. 8 for the ideal bedding arrangement).

B. Windows

Stick to washable cotton or synthetic window shades and/or washable cotton or fiberglass curtains. Avoid venetian blinds and draperies.

C. Floors

Avoid shaggy carpets.

D. Furniture

Use canvas, plastic, or leather upholstery; avoid all fabric-upholstered furniture.

E. Miscellaneous

1. Use washable paint or wallpaper on walls.

2. Avoid pictures and wall hangings.

3. Keep closets and all doors shut.

4. Store clothing in plastic zippered bags.

5. Avoid keeping dust catchers in the room, such as books, knickknacks, stuffed animals, and toys.

6. Do not use aerosols in your room.

7. Avoid perfumes, powders, flowers, and plants.

8. Keep pets out of your room.

9. Dust your room daily with a lamb's-wool duster. Wear a mask over your nose and mouth while dusting. Vacuuming spreads small dust particles and should be avoided. Air out the room after cleaning. For further cleaning details, see Chapter 8.

10. Remove plants from your bedroom or other rooms in which you spend a lot of time (they are dust catchers).

F. Heating

1. Electric heating or hot water is preferred over hot air ducts. If you have hot air heat, install an electrostatic filter.

2. Avoid electric fans (they stir up dust).

3. Filters and air conditioners are helpful. Investigate products carefully before purchasing to determine that they are truly effective.

4. Keep temperature 68° to 70° and humidity 40 to 60 percent.

G. Damp Areas (basement, cellar, laundry areas)

1. Dehumidifiers help to decrease mold growth.

2. Humidifiers and air conditioners can be a source of mold growth. They should be cleaned frequently with a disinfectant and dried thoroughly.

3. Demolding agents are helpful for treating cellars, summer dwellings, or other areas where mold is a problem. Demolding agents are usually applied by spraying a fine mist over the area to be treated. It is important to wear a mask while doing this, because the mist is irritating to the lungs. Demolding agents can be bought at a garden supply store. Can someone do this for you?

Crowds. We want you to go everywhere, but take care with crowds. If you see somebody sneezing or coughing, run in the other direction. If you do have to socialize with somebody with a respiratory infection, turn away quickly if they begin to cough and, most of all, do not shake hands or touch them. If you are exposed to somebody who coughed, wash your hands, because the virus on your hands which then may be lifted to the nose, eyes, or mouth, may infect you.

Mineral Oil

The use of mineral oil as a cathartic is not advisable. Small amounts can deposit in your lungs and give you lipoid pneumonia.

Choking

If you choke on food in public, put your hand to your throat in the international choking sign (Fig. 17); give your best therapeutic cough. If obstruction is severe and you have no help, use the following self-save technique. Make a fist with one hand and push the fist with the other hand as hard as possible into the middle of the area between your belly button and rib cage. Push up and in sharply. Repeat if necessary.

(Fig. 17) Heimlich International Choking Sign. Hand held to the throat.

Alternate technique: Bend over a high-backed chair, railing, or table edge. Press your abdomen into the edge with a quick movement. Repeat if necessary (Fig. 18).

Influenza and Pneumonia

Take appropriate vaccines—the influenza vaccine yearly, and Pneumovax, a protection against pneumococcal (a kind of bacterial) pneumonia, according to current recommendations.

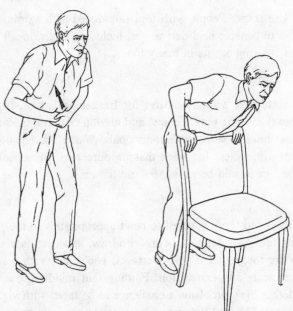

(Fig. 18) Heimlich Maneuver—Self-save Technique. Press your fist into your abdomen with a quick upward thrust. Repeat several times if necessary. Alternative Technique. Press upper abdomen onto the edge of a chair with quick movements. Repeat as necessary.

Exercise

Exercise may induce asthma or wheezing. Try to avoid activities that definitely cause severe wheezing, no matter what you do. However, two breaths of a bronchodilator spray just before exercise may end the entire problem. Cromolyn sodium may also be helpful. If you have this problem, be sure to tell your doctor rather than becoming sedentary.

Aspirin

Aspirin may induce asthma, especially in people who have nasal polyps. There are many good aspirin substitutes, such as acetaminophen. Use those. People with aspirin-induced asthma may also be sensitive to benzoic acid derivatives, including tartrazine. These are used as coloring agents in many foods.

Metabisulfites

Metabisulfites, a food additive for freshening lettuce, fruits, and potatoes (including potato chips) and used in restaurants, can induce severe asthma in susceptible individuals. Watch what you eat, and check the ingredient list when making purchases. Metabisulfites are also used in certain beers, wines, and liquors.

Stress

You want to teach yourself to react appropriately to the problems of your life. You don't want to withdraw, afraid to face up when things are tough; yet if you overreact, you're left with mental and physical scars and exhaustion. Finding that middle ground means considering life's problems a challenge to be faced with vigor and a stout heart. The next time stress is in the picture and you are terrified or furious, ask yourself, "Could I settle for being scared and angry?" Well, could you instead then be a little anxious and miffed—that's OK, too. Then ask yourself, did the whole thing really matter? If it matters, accept some stress.

There are some situations we can't avoid, but try not to stress yourself about things that don't really matter.

Glaucoma—Cataracts

If taking steroid hormones, see your eye doctor twice a year for early detection and treatment of these possible side effects.

A Daily Therapeutic Technique

Pulmonary toilette is a form of chest physical therapy coupled with the effective use of a bronchodilator. Its aim is to prevent or ameliorate bronchospasm and facilitate the removal of secretions. Begin with a hot drink. There's something about a hot drink that stirs things up. Follow this by inhaling a bronchodilator and moisture (e.g., steam) if prescribed for you. Next comes postural drainage. Use the positions which are most comfortable and practical for you. As you change each position, do a controlled therapeutic cough (previously described). Now is a good time to inhale beclomethasone or cromolyn if prescribed, since the bronchial tree is maximally cleared.

A regimen of pulmonary toilette is advised four times a day if you have excessive sputum production (or mucus secretion). Practically speaking, you may not be able to squeeze it all in. If you are away from home, you should have a hand nebulizer or MDI, and wherever you are, go to a quiet place, even if it is the ladies' or men's room, sit down, inhale your bronchodilator, and at least put your head down if you have sputum production, and try to give a good therapeutic cough. If you find that you feel exceptionally well after each postural drainage, you should try to commit yourself to a full regimen four times a day. If postural drainage helps, it is extremely important to do this full regimen at least in the morning on arising and in the evening before going to bed. Secretions pile up during the night, and the morning is frequently a difficult time for you. Allow yourself thirty minutes to complete the regimen. This is also a good time to add another glass or cup of hot liquid. By drinking two cups of hot liquid four times a day, you have your extra ration all in without giving it another thought. Do pulmonary toilette on an empty stomach.

We've come to the end of this chapter. You understand your problem as well as the treatment. You know about your medications and how to maintain and use all your equipment. You've learned how to manipulate some of your own drugs with permission, how to speak to your doctor intelligently, and how to do a physical examination on yourself and record your symptoms accurately and scientifically. You've learned to cope with factors in your life that may injure you and how to have a dust-free, hypo-allergenic home. You've learned a daily therapeutic pulmonary toilette regimen. This chapter requires concentration and rereading. The keynote to this chapter is understanding—your medicines as well as your symptoms. With understanding comes "living well" with COPD.

4

Body Business

It seems as though everyone these days is worrying about their diet —you should, too. Your nutritional concerns are very real and are related to more than just a good figure in a bathing suit. The kinds and quantity of food you consume may mean success or failure in your participation in an active and full life as described in this book. You eat plenty—right? You eat foods that are easy to prepare—right? Well, that's good. But what do you eat? Is your diet predominantly junk food, foods composed mainly of sugar and no other nutrients, or what we call delicious garbage—smoked, salty, fatty, or fried foods such as kielbasa, salami, hot dogs, french fries, and greasy fried chicken? You can't afford that, not and "live well." Here's why.

Recent investigations indicate that many patients with COPD are malnourished; even patients who have normal or excess weight may have below-normal muscle mass. Low muscle mass means poor strength and inability to be active. Studies have shown that individuals with COPD who have poor muscle mass also have weak respiratory muscles, with a markedly reduced ability to breathe deeply. It goes without saying that the ability to breathe deeply is an essential component of "living well." Furthermore, if your weight is normal, if your muscle mass is low, you have excess fat. An increase in fat weight means you must carry around unnecessary tissue that lends no strength to your body. You're already having enough trouble moving around; you don't need this added burden. Excess fat may be deposited in your coronary arteries as well as around your middle, resulting in heart disease as well as pulmonary disease.

Lower than normal fat weight means you have inadequate protection if you cannot eat for a few days or weeks or if you are unexpectedly exposed to the cold.

And what about some of the other things you eat, or don't eat? Inadequate carbohydrate means limitation of energy, including energy supply to your respiratory muscles.

Too much sodium intake means you'll be walking around with extra water weight, another added burden.

Inadequate calcium intake may result in a loss of bone tissue, leading to painful and debilitating fractures, most commonly in the back, hips, ribs, and wrists in a disease called osteoporosis.

A diet low in fiber may lead to miserable bowel movements, with chronic constipation and rectal pain.

The work your body must do to breathe—that's right, not to walk and talk, but to breathe—is six to ten times greater than that of a normal person (called increased *work of breathing).* If you want to have the energy and strength to "live well," you can see how complicated the problem is. It can't be done with junk foods and delicious garbage.

You need to make some type of realistic assessment of whether you are over- or underweight, over- or underfat, or whether you may have high or low lean body mass. This is not easy and can only be approximated with the tests which are ordinarily available to you. You need to have a wonderful, varied diet, and you need to achieve that with a minimum of energy expenditure. You need to have the strength to be able to buy the right foods and to eat right. That's going to take some study. It can be done. We're going to show you how. In this chapter we will discuss all major nutrients, summarize the latest theories on nutrition as it relates to your health, and disease. You will learn to formulate a sound diet, equip your kitchen, cook meals, and get your shopping done, all within the range of your physical capability. We will have special comments for those days when you don't feel well and your appetite is poor.

So be fashionable—join in the diet craze. By the end of this chapter you will be able to discuss diets with the best of them.

WHAT'S WHAT

Carbohydrates, eaten as sugar and starches, provide on-the-spot energy. There are two types: simple sugars such as table sugar, which if not used immediately are converted to fat, and complex carbohydrates such as those found in fruits, breads, and cereals. The latter are utilized slowly over a longer period of time, so the opportunities for immediate conversion to fat are less. A small amount of excess carbohydrate can be stored as a substance called glycogen (for emergencies), but the rest is converted to fat. It's important to have an adequate daily supply of complex carbohydrates.

Proteins, composed of substances called amino acids, and found in meat, fish, poultry, and some vegetables, are the building blocks of bone, blood, tendons, ligaments, muscles, and all the body cells. There are nine amino acids which the body cannot manufacture and therefore must be eaten daily. They are called essential amino acids. Animal proteins contain all the essential amino acids and therefore are called complete proteins. There's protein in vegetables, too, such as in soybeans, but vegetable proteins do not contain all the essential building blocks or amino acids and therefore are called incomplete proteins. Certain vegetables, such as rice and beans, "complement" each other and when eaten together result in the ingestion of complete protein. If you are missing one essential amino acid in your diet over a period of time, severe malnutrition will result. Excess proteins cannot be stored like carbohydrates and are converted to fat if they are not burned as energy.

Fats are oily substances such as are found in meat, salad oils, and dairy products such as cream, whole milk, and cheese. Fat provides the largest store of potential energy in the body. Once the body's small carbohydrate stores are used up, the rest of the energy must come from fat. Therefore, the longer the energy requirement (i.e., exercise) continues, the more likely it is that the body's energy is coming from burned fat. Excess fats are metabolized by the liver and then carried into the bloodstream. All excessive food intake, including alcohol, results in the manufacture of fat.

Carbohydrates and protein contain four calories per gram. Fats contain nine calories per gram. Three ounces equal one hundred grams.

Fiber, found mainly in certain vegetables, fruit, whole wheat and bran cereals, is a nondigestible food element. Fiber is not absorbed. Fiber adds bulk to bowel movements, making them softer and more easily passed by binding water and fats, including dietary cholesterol. Waste material leaves the body faster in a high-fiber diet. People who eat high-fiber diets generally have less constipation, may have lower cholesterol, and possibly a lower incidence of cancer of the colon.

Minerals are a part of every cell and especially are associated with the conversion of food to energy. *Sodium,* the principal content of table salt, is an essential ingredient in the chemical reactions that take place in the body fluids outside the cells. However, very little sodium, probably about two grams a day (one teaspoon or much less) is required by the body. A regular diet in which sodium is used in cooking but not added to the food upon eating usually contains four grams of sodium a day. Excess sodium may result in water retention, increased work for the heart, and high blood pressure. The latter contributes to heart disease and stroke. *Potassium* is an essential ingredient of chemical reactions that take place within the body's cells and is a food constituent found in meat, bananas, oranges, prunes, and other vegetables and fruits. With normal kidneys there is no disorder from excess intake of potassium, but lack of potassium causes weakness, muscle cramps, and abnormal heart rhythm. *Calcium* is found in certain vegetables, cereal products, and particularly milk and cheese protein. It is the body's most abundant mineral, and combines with the mineral phosphorus in the formation of bones and teeth. It is also important in the reactions that make muscles function. Your heart would not be able to pump without sodium, potassium, and calcium.

Vitamins are, as their name describes, minute amounts of food elements vital to life. They do not supply energy or contribute to body weight. They cannot be manufactured by the body, so they must be supplied in the diet, and they are absolutely essential for most body functions. Vitamins are widely distributed in meats, fish, poultry, vegetables, and fruits, along with minerals. Without vitamins the body could not make new tissue, fight infection, or regulate energy production.

Water is a non-energy-supplying liquid nutrient essential to life, comprising approximately 60 percent of our body weight and functioning as the body's foremost transport medium for nutrients, gases, and waste products. Under normal circumstances two and a half quarts of water a day are utilized, but that includes the liquid ingested as food. Man can live a long time without food (provided he has normal body muscle and fat), but only a few days without water.

Alcohol, as found in wine, beer, and liquor, is a food which supplies energy but has no vitamins, minerals, protein, fat, or carbohydrate. While small amounts of about one ounce a day or less may in some instances lower the blood cholesterol, excess amounts lead to deterioration of the liver and nervous system, including the brain.

Caffeine is a drug found in coffee, tea, cocoa, and many carbonated beverages. In low doses (e.g. the amount in, one cup of coffee) caffeine may increase concentration. In higher doses caffeine causes restlessness, nervousness, and insomnia, raises the pulse rate and possibly the blood pressure. When people consume a lot of caffeine, their heart rate goes up out of proportion to the amount of exercise. Therefore, they tire more easily and can do less.

WHAT'S NEW

Now that you've become a minor expert with the major foodstuffs, let us dazzle you with some of the new discoveries in nutrition as they relate to your health.

The Exercise-Fat Connection. Recently two separate groups of patients were put on identical reducing diets. One group entered into an exercise training program exactly as described in Chapter 5. The other group remained sedentary. The weight loss for both groups was identical. The group who remained sedentary lost 50 percent fat and 50 percent muscle mass. The group who dieted *and* exercised lost about 95 percent fat and 5 percent muscle mass. If you are a sedentary person who loses and gains weight and suffers from the "yo-yo syndrome," then when you are on the down "yo," you lose fat and muscle, and when you are on the up "yo," you replace muscle with fat. With each diet binge you will grow weaker and will have a lower muscle mass and a higher fat mass. *That's bad.*

The Vitamin-Cancer Connection. The National Research Council (NRC), a scientific advisory group to our federal government, has issued a report entitled "Diet, Nutrition and Cancer," urging us to eat more foods containing vitamins A and C, which may lower the risk of some cancers. Beta carotene is the safe and powerful precursor of vitamin A found in certain fruits and vegetables. Even heavy smokers reduce their risk of lung cancer by increasing their intake of these natural foods. In other studies heavy smokers who ate small amounts of beta carotene were four times as likely to have cancer as those heavy smokers who ate large amounts. Vitamin A seems to help the delicate cells lining the bronchial tree to reproduce and repair themselves in such a way that they are able to continue their normal functions. Without vitamin A the cells become dry and hard and show changes which resemble those caused by tumor-producing chemicals. Overdoses of vitamin A, on the other hand, can cause severe liver damage and injuries to the brain and nervous system. Therefore, increasing the intake of vitamin A by tablets is not recommended. When you eat vitamin A in foods or in its natural form, beta carotene, the body controls the rate of conversion and there are no toxic side effects. Try to eat a daily source of natural vitamin A, or beta carotene.

The evidence for vitamin C as a possible cancer preventer is compelling. Vitamin C stops the formation of nitrosamines, a group of substances that cause cancer in animals. The National Research Council pointed out in studies that they reviewed that those population groups observed who ate fruits and vegetables containing vitamin C had lower rates of stomach and esophageal cancer. A daily source of vitamin C is important.

The NRC has made further interim suggestions as their research continues. Americans have been advised to avoid excessive alcohol intake, minimize eating smoked or salt-cured foods such as ham and pickled herring, lower fat intake, and to include whole-grain or high-fiber cereals as part of their daily diet.

The Calcium Link. We used to think that osteoporosis, or weak, thin bones that tend to get small fractures, as described in a previous section, and periodontal disease, disease of the gums which results in the teeth being loose and falling out, were diseases of older or middle-aged people. They are, but now we know that their beginnings are rooted in the young who have sedentary lives and who possibly have a poor calcium intake. We used to think that milk was a children's food. It's no longer so. Adults need an ample intake of calcium throughout their lifetime, coupled with exercise, as the best means now known of lessening the risk of osteoporosis and periodontal disease. It's long been known that steroid hormones such as prednisone, at times very necessary medications for people with COPD, can also cause the breakdown of bone and contribute to osteoporosis. This makes a high intake of calcium coupled with exercise seem all the more important, since vigorous upright exercise, such as walking briskly, tends to stimulate new bone formation, and vigorous exercise actually reversed the bone loss and muscle loss found in our astronauts due to weightlessness. One final note: Smoking and excessive alcohol intake may also contribute to osteoporosis.

"Good" and "Bad" Cholesterol. Most people know there are two kinds of fat—saturated, as is found in fatty meats and cream and animal products, and unsaturated, as is found in vegetable oil. What's new is that all excess foods, including alcohol, are metabolized by the liver into fat and contribute to the formation of low-density lipoprotein, or LDL, and are then carried into the blood-

stream. It's postulated that large quantities of LDL in the bloodstream injure the lining of blood vessels, especially in the coronary arteries, and that's how arteriosclerosis may begin. Unsaturated fats, unless they are eaten in excess, tend to lower the manufacture of LDL, or bad cholesterol, by the liver, and exercise tends to favor the manufacture of what's called high-density lipoprotein, or HDL, the good cholesterol, for HDL does not result in deposits in the coronary arteries. In fact, exercise can actually raise the ratio of HDL to LDL. It comes down to this—if you walk, walk, walk, and eat right, you might have more good cholesterol than bad. And good cholesterol is the kind worth having!

The Fiber-Cancer Connection. Populations that eat very high quantities of fibrous foods have extremely large stools and very low rates of cancer of the bowel. How can that be? Scientists are not sure but postulate that when bacteria "sit around" they may make low-level cancer-producing compounds. By eating fiber along with fluids you might be fighting cancer as well as constipation.

Good and Not-So-Good Starches. A high simple sugar load results in an outpouring of insulin from the pancreas. Insulin is quite efficient at getting sugar metabolized and deposited as fat if it's not burned quickly. It also tends to overshoot slightly, causing the blood sugar to drop, resulting in hunger. Haven't you had that happen? You eat a candy bar because you're hungry, but shortly after you're finished, you're hungrier than ever. This may set up a vicious cycle of overeating and a binge on sweets. Since starches, or as we described them, complex sugars, are metabolized more slowly, insulin levels tend not to rise rapidly. Recently, however, it's been discovered that all starchy foods are not alike, even when the starch is in a single food prepared in different ways (e.g., the wheat in pasta as opposed to that in bread), with some starches causing more of a blood sugar rise than others. We have divided starches into three groups based on low, medium, or high blood sugar responses. In the lowest or most desirable group are apples, oranges, milk, yogurt, dried legumes (beans, chick-peas, lentils, black-eyed peas), sweet potatoes, yams, spaghetti, bran, and oatmeal. In the middle group are raisins, bananas, beets, new potatoes, bread, shredded wheat, rice, and sweet corn. In the highest group are parsnips, carrots, instant potatoes, and cornflakes.

As regards simple sugars, here are some surprises. The blood sugar response to fructose (fruit sugar, corn syrup) is in the very lowest group, sucrose is in the middle, and honey (the darling of food faddists) is in the highest group, along with glucose and maltose.

To avoid a binge choose foods from the lowest group to help alleviate this problem.

The Tromsø-Coffee Connection. In a recent study in Tromsø, Norway, thousands of people were questioned about their coffee consumption, which was then plotted against their blood cholesterol. Cholesterol rose significantly with each cup of coffee, including decaffeinated. Coffee may actually "help" the liver make cholesterol! Therefore, we can't recommend more than one cup per day. Look into delicious natural cereal beverages such as Pero, Cafix, Bambu, and Postum.

You should now be armed with the facts—a veritable whiz. It's clear we think you shouldn't diet unless you're willing to exercise. You need the best muscle mass you can get. You don't want to be too thin or too fat. You don't want to carry around extra water and eat rich, salty foods which may increase the risk of hypertension and heart attack, or smoked, cured foods which may increase the risk of cancer. You can't afford the consequences of delicious garbage and junk food. You want a diet high in fiber, foods containing calcium and vitamins A and C, and complex carbohydrates with adequate high-quality protein and not too much fat. Where can you find such a special diet? Right in this chapter, of course. But first, we have to do some self-analysis.

WEIGHT, FAT, AND MUSCLE

1. Compare your weight with that of the Metropolitan Life Insurance Company 1983 weight tables* printed below.

MEN

Height	Small Frame	Medium Frame	Large Frame
5' 2"	128–134	131–141	138–150
5' 3"	130–136	133–143	140–153
5' 4"	132–138	135–145	142–156
5' 5"	134–140	137–148	144–160
5' 6"	136–142	139–151	146–164
5' 7"	138–145	142–154	149–168
5' 8"	140–148	145–157	152–172
5' 9"	142–151	148–160	155–176
5'10"	144–154	151–163	158–180
5'11"	146–157	154–166	161–184
6' 0"	149–160	157–170	164–188
6' 1"	152–164	160–174	168–192
6' 2"	155–168	164–178	172–197
6' 3"	158–172	167–182	176–202
6' 4"	162–176	171–187	181–207

WOMEN

Height	Small Frame	Medium Frame	Large Frame
4'10"	102–111	109–121	118–131
4'11"	103–113	111–123	120–134
5' 0"	104–115	113–126	122–137
5' 1"	106–118	115–129	125–140
5' 2"	108–121	118–132	128–143
5' 3"	111–124	121–135	131–147
5' 4"	114–127	124–138	134–151
5' 5"	117–130	127–141	137–155
5' 6"	120–133	130–144	140–159
5' 7"	123–136	133–147	143–163
5' 8"	126–139	136–150	146–167
5' 9"	129–142	139–153	149–170
5'10"	132–145	142–156	152–173

| 5′11″ | 135–148 | 145–159 | 155–176 |
| 6′ 0″ | 138–151 | 148–162 | 158–179 |

* For people in shoes and wearing five pounds of indoor clothing for men, three pounds for women.

How do you rate? Circle one: normal weight, overweight, underweight.

2. What's Fat

Pinch the skin at a point exactly one half the distance between the shoulder and the elbow on the back of the arm. Do not include muscle, which is deeper and firmer. Pinch three-quarters to one inch in from the edge of skin. This is the triceps skin fold. How far apart are your fingers?

TRICEPS SKIN FOLD
Normal Range

	Inches	Centimeters	You
MEN	3/8–5/8	1.0–1.5	___
WOMEN	1/2–3/4	1.2–1.9	___

How do you rate? Circle one: normal fat, overfat, underfat.

3. What's Muscle

To determine muscle we must first measure the mid upper arm circumference. Take a measuring tape and measure the circumference of your arm at the exact point at which you took your pinch to answer question 2. Check the chart below.

MID UPPER ARM CIRCUMFERENCE
Normal Range

	Inches	Centimeters	You
MEN	10–13	25.5–33	___
WOMEN	10–12½	25.5–32	___

The upper arm circumference includes both fat and muscle. To know what's muscle, derive your mid upper arm muscle circumference as follows:

a. Multiply the triceps skin fold (your answer for question 2) times three.

b. Subtract the answer in *a* from the mid upper arm circumference (your answer for question 3).

c. Compare with the following table.

MID UPPER ARM MUSCLE CIRCUMFERENCE
Normal Range

	Inches	Centimeters	You
MEN	9–11½	23–29	_____
WOMEN	8–10½	20–27	_____

How do you rate this time? Normal muscle, athletically muscled, undermuscled.

4. What's your final diagnosis? Check the answers that apply.

overweight_____	underweight_____	normal weight_____
overfat_____	underfat_____	normal fat_____
athletically muscled_____	undermuscled_____	normal muscle_____

These are rough tests. Scientifically accurate estimations of body composition require underwater weighing or other techniques which are as yet being developed for pulmonary patients. Still, these rough guides with subsequent retesting by you can help you formulate the number of calories you should be eating and allow you to follow your progress toward a normal body composition. We have formulated the proportions of proteins, carbohydrates, and fats for you.

We find that pulmonary patients, aside from those with normal weight muscle and fat, fall into one of the following several general categories. In fact, if you don't, take the test again. (If you just can't manage the pinch and the tape measure, use the weight chart alone.) Now let's examine the results of your body composition study. You found:

1. Normal weight, excess fat, and low muscle mass.

Analysis: Sedentary—wrong food.

Solution: You need to exercise and lift light weights in order to increase muscle. Our diet will allow you to prepare food easily and insure that your intake is low in fat and has adequate vitamins and protein. Your present consumption of calories is fine. Adapting to our diet, count about fifteen calories per pound of ideal body weight.

2. Overweight, overfat, and high-normal to low muscle mass.

Analysis: Sedentary, eat too much—wrong food.

Solution: Exercise, including lifting light weights, to reduce fat and maintain or improve muscle mass. Calorie count for males: 1500; females: 1200. Our diet should provide adequate protein to improve or maintain muscle mass while losing fat.

3. Underweight, underfat, and low muscle mass.

Analysis: Work of breathing significantly increased, intake of calories and protein insufficient, sedentary.

Solution: Try to increase activity by walking and light weight lifting to improve muscle mass (inactive people cannot make muscle). Increase intake of protein to provide building blocks of muscles as you increase your activity. Calculate calories as follows: ideal weight times fifteen calories per pound for moderate activity; ideal weight times twenty calories per pound for high-stress conditions. Don't get discouraged. Much research still needs to be done on your problem.

This book seeks to open up new worlds of choices and ranges of interests, but not when it comes to the food you eat. If you want to have a healthy *corps* (or body), you have to eat a healthy core of foods. Here's a real, honest-to-goodness, no-gimmick, miracle diet based on the best and the latest we could find in the scientific literature and in recommendations from the federal government.

Does that sound boring? Can you have a miracle diet without a miracle food? You can't, you say. We *promised* you'd be as trendy as the best of them, and we deliver on our promises—your miracle food is broccoli.

To find out why, read on.

THE HEALTHY CORE DIET

An easy way to psych out any diet is to divide it into basic food groups. We've done that here, but with our own special categories.

1. High-calcium contributors: including fat-free milk, yogurt, low-cholesterol cheese, frogurt (or frozen yogurt), canned sardines and salmon with their bones, and *broccoli*. Four or more portions equivalent to 1,000 milligrams or more of calcium per day.

2. Cancer-fighting foods containing vitamins A and C: including grapefruit (especially pink), oranges, strawberries, watermelon, cantaloupe, brussels sprouts, cauliflower, sweet peppers, spinach, tomatoes, carrots, sweet potatoes, and *broccoli*. Three to five servings, supplying vitamin A (minimum daily requirement, 5,000 units per day for men and 4,000 units for women) and vitamin C (minimum daily requirement, 60 milligrams per day).

3. Energy elevators: including breads, cereals, pasta, macaroni, rice, and beans. Three to four or more servings per day (125 grams of complex carbohydrate = minimum).

4. Muscle builders (proteins): including meats, fish, poultry, peanut butter, low-fat cottage cheese, and egg whites. Two or more portions a day to equal about one gram for every pound of your ideal body weight in kilograms (= body weight divided by 2.2). With increased stress, however, protein requirements also increase, as high as 1.5 to 2 grams for every pound of ideal body weight in kilograms.

5. Fiber foods: including bran, potato skins, carrots, brussels sprouts, cauliflower, bananas, cabbage, corn, oranges, raw apples, pears, dried apricots, high-fiber cereals, whole-grain, long-cooking cereals, and *broccoli*. No particular minimum daily requirement has been established. Try for twenty or more grams of fiber per day.

Some foods actually cross over several categories. For instance, low-fat milk provides high-quality protein as well as being dense in calcium. For clarity's sake, we have generally avoided listing foods under more than one category but rather in the area in which they make their most important contribution to you. Isn't broccoli a knockout? It's loaded with beta carotene and vitamin C, as well as calcium and fiber, and there's some vegetable protein and carbohydrate there, too.

How to know *exactly* your requirement for calories, carbohydrates, fats, and protein? That's difficult. Your doctor is in the best position to help. If you are very thin, quite malnourished, and undermuscled as determined by your test, and quite short of breath all the time, it may be best to arrange an assessment by a nutritionist trained to make sophisticated estimates of your body composition and needs.

The Healthy Core Diet is high in complex carbohydrates (40 to 55 percent of daily calories), has little or no simple sugar, is low in fat (25 to 30 percent of total daily calories) and cholesterol (less than 300 milligrams a day), has adequate protein for moderate stress (20 to 27 percent daily), and is high in fiber, low in alcohol (less than 60 milligrams a day or none), and high in calcium (1,000-plus milligrams a day), vitamins A (15,000 units-plus) and C (250 milligrams-plus). It also contains all other essential vitamins and minerals according to the Natural Research Council's recommended dietary allowances.

Fifteen hundred calories may not be enough for you to eat, according to the analysis of your body composition and stress factors. Therefore, we've adapted the Healthy Core diet to calorie counts of 2,000, 2,500, and 3,000. On the other hand, you may be someone who needs to lose weight, so we've also subtracted from the diet to produce a 1,200 calorie regimen which still maintains that healthy *corps.*

Get in the habit of eating the same breakfast and lunch each day until you really understand good nutrition. When you do make variations, retain the principles of the Healthy Core diet. Eat chicken or fish five or six times a week and lean red meat one or two times a week. Use the diet exchange charts that follow to help with your choices.

If you are not undermuscled or subject to increased stress, you

HEALTHY CORE DIET: 1500 CALORIES

	Calories	Protein gms	Carbohydrate gms	Fiber gms	Chol. mgs Tot. / Fat gms	Ca mgs	A units	C mgs	Sodium mgs
Breakfast									
All-Bran, 1 oz.	110	3.0	22	9.0	$\frac{0}{1.0}$	16	1,000	12.0	320
Skim milk, 1 cup	90	9.0	13	0	$\frac{0}{1.0}$	240	400	2.4	128
1/2 pink grapefruit, 4 in.	50	0.5	12	0.2	$\frac{0}{0}$	16	440	44.0	1
Bread, whole wheat, 1 slice	60	2.4	11	0.4	$\frac{trace}{0.7}$	23	trace	trace	121
Coffee, 1 cup	2	0	0.5	0	0	7	0	0	12
Lunch									
Low-fat cheese, Lite-Line, processed, 3 slices	113	15.7	2.25	0	$\frac{23}{4.5}$	350	0	0	900*
Peanut butter, 1 tbsp.	94	4.4	3.2	.36	$\frac{0}{8}$	12	0	0	20
Pita bread, small, whole wheat	80	4	15	0.4	$\frac{trace}{0.3}$	16	0 trace	0 trace	0
Carrot, 1 large	42	1.1	9.7	1.0	$\frac{0}{0.2}$	37	11,000	9	47

Food									
Pepper, lettuce, tomato, mixed	40	1.5	6.0	0.6	0 / 0	14	600	40	8
Apple, 2 in.	97	0.3	21.7	1.5	0 / 0.9	10	140	6	1
Dinner									
Poultry, white meat, 3½ oz.	166	31.6	0	0	69 / 3.4	11	60	2	50
Sweet potato, baked, 1 medium	141	2.1	32.5	0.9	0 / 0.5	40	8,100	24	12
Lettuce or salad	14	1.2	2.5	0.5	0 / 0	35	970	2	9
Dressing (oil & vinegar), 1 tbsp.	79.6	0	1.0	0	0 / 8.4	2	trace	trace	200*
Broccoli, 3 stalks	78	9.3	13.5	4.5	0 / 0.9	264	7,500	270	30
Orange, 3 in.	73	1.5	18.3	0.8	0 / 0.3	62	300	80	2
Snack									
Popcorn, 2 cups	108	3.6	21.4	0.3	0 / 0.7	2	0	0	0
Skim milk, 1 cup	90	9.0	13	0	0 / 1.0	240	400	2.4	128
TOTALS	1527	100.2	218.5	20.46	92 / 31.8	1397	30,910	491.8	1991.4

*For very-low-sodium diets, use low-cholesterol, low-sodium cheeses, and make salad dressing from oil and vinegar without salt.

MODIFICATIONS OF HEALTHY CORE DIET TO VARYING CALORIE COUNTS

Calories:	1200	1500	2000	2500	3000
Breakfast					
All-Bran, 1 oz.	x	x	x	x	x
Skim milk, 1 cup	x	x	x	x	x
1/2 grapefruit (pink)	x	x	x	x	x
Bread, whole wheat, 1 slice	x	x	x	x	
Coffee, tea, etc.	x	x	x	x	x
Large roll, whole wheat			one	two	three
Raisins, 1 Tbsp.					
Lunch					
Low-fat cheese: Lite-Line	3 slices	3 slices	3 slices	3 slices	3 slices
Pita, small, whole wheat	x	x	x	x	x
Carrot, 1 large	x		x	x	x
Peanut butter		1 tbsp.	2 tbsp.	3 tbsp.	3 tbsp.
Vegetables, raw			x	x	x
Apple	1/2, 2-in.	2 in.	x	4 in.	4 in.
Tea, cereal beverage	x	x	x	x	x
Large roll, whole wheat					x
Tuna			1/2 cup	1/2 cup	1 cup
Mayonnaise			1 tbsp.	1tbsp.	3 tbsp.
Dinner					
Poultry, white meat	3½ oz.	3½ oz.	3½ oz.	3½ oz.	7 oz.
Sweet potato	½	1	1	1	1
Salad	x	x	x	x	x
Salad dressing	1 tbsp.	1 tbsp.	1 tbsp.	1 tbsp.	1 tbsp.
Salad oil				2 tbsp.	2 tbsp.
Broccoli, 3 stalks	x	x	x	x	x
Orange, 3 in.	x	x	x	x	x
Snacks					
Popcorn	1 cup	2 cups	2 cups	2 cups	2 cups
Skim milk, 1 cup	x	x	x	x	x
Fruit				1 large	2 large

may require less protein. Excessive protein intake results in the loss of calcium in the urine. Check with your doctor.

FOOD EXCHANGES

FRUITS AND VEGETABLES CONTAINING VITAMINS A AND C

Food	Calories	Vitamin A I.U.	Vitamin C mgm.
Fruits			
Apricots, dried, 9 medium	85	3,500	4
Cantaloupe, half, 5 in.	80	9,240	90
Grapefruit, pink, half	50	540	44
Oranges, one, 2 5/8 in.	65	260	66
Papaya, 1 cup cubes	89	2,450	78
Peaches, 1 medium	40	1,330	7
Strawberries, raw whole, 1 cup	55	90	151
Watermelon, 4-by-8-in. wedge	110	2,510	30
Vegetables			
Asparagus, 1 cup cuts, tips	30	1,310	38
Beans, snap, 1 cup	30	680	15
Broccoli, medium stalk	45	4,500	162
Brussels sprouts, 7–8	55	810	135
Cabbage, 1 cup	30	190	48
Carrots, 1 cup cross-cut	50	16,280	9
Cauliflower, 1 cup	93	80	69
Collards, 1 cup	65	14,820	144

Kale, 1 cup	45	9,130	102
Lettuce, 1 cup shredded	10	1,050	68
Peas, 1 cup	150	1,170	13
Peppers, sweet, 1 pod	15	310	94
Potatoes, 1, 1/2 lb., baked	145	Trace	31
Pumpkin, canned, 1 cup	80	15,680	12
Spinach, 1 cup	40	14,580	50
Squash, winter, 1 cup baked & mashed	130	8,610	27
Sweet potatoes, 1, medium, baked	160	9,230	25
Tomatoes, raw, 4 oz.	25	1,110	28
Turnip greens, 1 cup	30	8,270	68

Unless specified, values are for raw fruits and cooked vegetables. Data from U.S. Department of Agriculture Home and Garden Bulletin No. 72, *Nutritive Value of Foods,* revised April 1981.

SOURCES OF CALCIUM

	Calcium, Milligrams	Calories
Nonfat, fortified milk, 1 cup	359	105
Sardines (Atlantic), canned in oil, 8 medium	354	311
Skim milk, 1 cup	298	81
Whole milk, 1 cup	298	161
Yogurt (from skim milk), 1 cup	293	122
Canned, evaporated milk, 1/2 cup minus 1 tbsp.	252	137
American cheddar cheese, 1 oz. (a 1-in. cube)	211	112

SOURCES OF CALCIUM CONTINUED

	Calcium, Milligrams	Calories
Creamed cottage cheese, 1 cup	211	239
Canned salmon (pink, with bones), 2/5 cup	196	141
Dandelion greens, raw, 1/2 cup	187	45
Collard greens, cooked, 1/2 cup	152	29
Low-fat cottage cheese, 1 cup	138	163
Tofu, 3 1/2 oz.	128	72
Broccoli, 1 stalk, 5 1/2 in. long	103	32
Spinach, cooked, 1/2 cup	83	21
Green beans, 1 cup	62	31
Dry, nonfat milk powder, 1 tbsp.	49	14
Oysters, canned (solid + liquid), 3 1/2 oz.	28	76
Brazil nuts, 4 medium	28	97
Almonds (unsalted), 9–10 nuts	25	60
Whole wheat bread, 1 slice	23	56
English walnuts, 8–15 halves	12	98

Reprinted with permission of *Working Woman* magazine. Source for data: *Food Values of Portions Commonly Used,* 12th ed. revised by Charles Frederick Church and Helen Nichols Church (Philadelphia: J. B. Lippincott, 1975).

Low-Fat, Low-Cholesterol, High-Protein Exchanges (meat skinned, cooked, visible fat removed):

Lean beef

Lean veal

Lean lamb

Poultry except duck

Fish except shellfish

Low-fat cheese, including cottage cheese

A combination of 1 cup cooked rice with ½ cup cooked beans (e.g., kidney beans, lentils, lima beans, etc.)—3½ oz.

How to Add Calories

Bread, 1 slice—56
Popcorn, 1 cup—54
Low-fat cottage cheese, ½ cup—100
Rice, 1 cup—221
Fruit, 1 large—133
Kidney beans, raw, ½ cup—343
Bagel—125
Salmon or tunafish, water-packed, ¼ cup—58
Frozen yogurt (frogurt), 3 oz.—136
Weight Watchers' chocolate treat or frozen yogurt bar—100
Peanut butter, 1 tbsp.—94
Vegetable oil, 1 tbsp.—125
Fleischmann's Egg Beaters or similar, equivalent to 2 eggs—60

HEALTHY CORE SHOPPING LIST

We've done the thinking for you. We think it's nice to have someone to do that, especially at first. We've given you a shopping list for the first week. The proportions are for one person. The meat, however, is a two-week supply. Does that sound peculiar? Here's our grand plan: Five nights each week, cook one more portion than you need and freeze immediately in a plastic heat-sealed boilable/freezable bag. Label it with a felt-tip pen. The second week you'll only have to boil the bag. We suggest you cook five nights a week. Two nights a week eat salad and high-quality, reduced-calorie frozen meals (may not be advisable with very low sodium diets) or eat out (see Chap. 10, "Leisure, Work, and Travel"). If you're on the 3000-calorie diet, you get to eat two frozen meals. Stick to the Healthy Core diet as outlined. In a few weeks you can make your own adjustments. Comfort yourself by thinking of all the aisles you don't have to go down anymore.

FIRST WEEK HEALTHY CORE DIET
SHOPPING LIST FOR ONE
(Two Weeks' Meat Supply)

Calories	1200	1500	2000	2500	3000
Produce					
Grapefruit (pink), 4	X	X	X	X	X
Oranges, 3 in., 7	X	X	X	X	X
Fruits, small—2 in., 7	X	X	X		
Fruits, large—4 in., 7				X	X
Tomatoes, 3	X	X	X	X	X
Lettuce, 1	X	X	X	X	X
Peppers, 4	X	X	X	X	X
Carrots, 7	X	X	X	X	X
Sweet potatoes, medium	3	5	5	5	5
Broccoli, 2 large bunches	X	X	X	X	X
Meat					
Chicken breasts, whole	3	3	3	3	6
Lean ground beef	1/2 lb.	1/2 lb.	1/2 lb.	1/2 lb.	1 lb.
Fish	1/2 lb.	1/2 lb.	1/2 lb.	1/2 lb.	1 lb.
Dairy					
Cottage cheese, 1% fat	X	X	X	X	X
Skim milk (1 gal.) or equiv. powder	X	X	X	X	X
Cheese (Lite-Line or sim.) 2 12-slice packages	X	X	X	X	X
Baked Goods					
Bread, whole wheat	X	X			
Pita, (small, whole wheat) 7	X	X			
Large rolls or bagels, whole wheat, 14			X	X	X
Other					
Oil (unsaturated)			X	X	X
Popcorn kernels	X	X	X	X	X

All-Bran (or similar)	X	X	X	X	X
Spices as needed	X	X	X	X	X
Raisins			X	X	X
Salad dressing, Italian type (not sugared)	X	X	X	X	X
Canned					
Stewed tomatoes	X	X	X	X	X
Low-sodium bouillon	X	X	X	X	X
Beverages					
Tea, cereal beverage, etc.	X	X	X	X	X
Frozen Foods					
2 weeks: Main dishes (Lean Cuisine, Weight Watchers, etc.)	4	4	4	4	8
Broccoli (if fresh not available)					

Comments

If milk produces gas, bloating, or abdominal cramps, you may have lactose intolerance. The solution lies in adding LactAid, an enzyme which digests the lactose for you. If it is not available at your drug store, call 1-800-257-8650, the LactAid Hot Line, LactAid Inc., Pleasantville, N.J.

We've included a container of low-fat cottage cheese to use instead of butter.

Now you have the healthy, essential core we've been referring to right at your fingertips. Let's go on to your next task—getting the meals ready.

Cooking Lessons

All the recipes in this section use the principles of the Healthy Core diet and conservation of energy in the kitchen (described in detail in Chap. 8). Why don't you skip ahead and read the section entitled "COE in the Kitchen" right now?

We'll begin with a company meal. This menu will illustrate the principles we discuss in Chapter 8 as well as in this chapter, and being able to cook for company or a special person is important if you want to "live well." You can't cook? We can't either. The ability to cook, in the ordinary sense of the word, has little to do with eating right.

LE MENU (THE MENU)

Soupe à l'oignon gratinée (Onion soup with baked cheese crouton)

Coq au vin (Chicken with wine) (If alcohol isn't for you, leave the wine out and don't change the name.)

Salade verte (Green salad)

Chocolate mousse (Creamy pudding)

Cappuccino (Coffee alternative drink with foamed milk topped with cinnamon)

Here's your shopping list:

COMPANY MEAL FOR TWO SHOPPING LIST

Low-fat, low-cholesterol Swiss cheese, 1/4 lb.

Cup-a-Soup, onion, 1 box

Holland rusk, 1 pkg.

Chicken breast, 3 halves

Flour

Low-sodium instant broth and seasoning, 1 box

Wine, red, dry, 3/4 cup

Thyme

Garlic powder

Bay leaf

Whole potatoes, 1 can

Whole onions, 1 can

Loose-leaf lettuce, 1

Vegetable spray

Oil

Vinegar

Mustard powder

Skim milk powder

Coffee substitute drink (Pero, Cafix, Postum, etc.)

Unflavored gelatin

Low-fat (1%) cottage cheese

Reduced-calorie chocolate pudding mix (with NutraSweet)

Low-fat yogurt, plain, small carton

SOUPE À L'OIGNON GRATINÉE

Tear one thin slice of low-fat, low-cholesterol Swiss cheese into tiny pieces and divide between each of 2 soup crocks or bowls. Add one package of instant dried onion Cup-a-Soup to each crock or bowl.

Take 2 Holland rusks and put a generous slice of low-cholesterol Swiss cheese on the top of each. Put the Holland rusk with the cheese on top into your toaster oven on a piece of tinfoil, curling the end of the tinfoil up to make a small handle so you can slide it out easily. Turn on the broiler, and when the cheese melts, remove from the oven.

Add ¾ cup boiling water to each crock or bowl and stir well. The cheese will melt and make the soup creamy and delicious. Slide the cheese-covered crouton off the tinfoil and onto the top of the soup. Be ready to eat immediately.

To make this dish properly, get everything ready in advance. Have the crouton in the oven and torn cheese and the soup base in the crock. Do the final steps of adding boiling water, stirring well, and sliding the crouton on top just before your coq au vin is ready for eating.

COQ AU VIN

Put 3 pieces of chicken (one extra to freeze) in an electric frying pan which has been sprayed with vegetable spray. Warm through and/or brown slightly. Sprinkle with a very good handful of flour, coating all sides of the chicken lightly. Rub the flour in with the back of a spoon and use a wad of paper toweling to turn the chicken over as you sprinkle the flour on. Leave the breast side, or the "up" side, of your chicken down for the first half of the cooking time. Sprinkle garlic powder lightly all over the chicken (add more later if you like). Add 1½ cups boiling water to 2 packages of low-sodium instant broth and seasoning mix. Stir and add to the chicken. Add half as much again dry red wine. You can use a disposable cup as a measuring cup. Put in 2 good pinches or shakes of thyme. (Caution: Don't overdo. Thyme is a powerful herb.) Add a bay leaf in the corner. Cover and cook at a slow simmer for about 45 minutes or until fork tender. Come back once midway. Stir the sauce around and turn the chicken pieces over. At that time add 6 small, whole, canned potatoes and 6 whole, canned onions.

SALADE VERTE

Tear the leaves from loose-leaf lettuce with your hands and dry off with a paper towel after washing the lettuce. Put in each of 2 bowls and chill. Add the following dressing to each of the bowls just before serving.

Vinaigrette Dressing: Mix 2 tablespoons of oil and 1 tablespoon of wine vinegar with a liberal amount of garlic powder, pepper, and 2 shakes of dried mustard in a covered jar. Shake well. Refrigerate. Make vinaigrette dressing while the chicken is cooking or earlier in the day.

CAPPUCINO

Pour ½ cup skim milk powder and 1 cup boiling water into blender. Blend vigorously for a few moments until there is foam on top of the milk.

Have 2 cups, each with a heaping teaspoon of coffee alternative powder ready.

Just before serving, add ½ cup boiling water to each cup and ½ cup warmed milk. Take a big spoon and remove the foamed milk (which tends to stay behind naturally) and drop it on the top. Sprinkle lightly with cinnamon. *Voilà!* Cappucino.

CHOCOLATE MOUSSE

Early on that special day—

Add to blender: ½ packet plain gelatin and 1 tablespoon hot water from sink to moisten gelatin. Add ½ cup powdered skim milk. Pour in 1½ cups boiling water and blend on lowest possible speed for 30 seconds.

Sprinkle one envelope (4-serving size) reduced-calorie chocolate pudding with NutraSweet over the mixture and blend again at low speed for 30 seconds. Add 2 oz. (or ½ cup) low-fat yogurt and 2 oz. (or ½ cup) of low-fat cottage cheese.

Blend again until thoroughly mixed. Pour into wine glasses and chill (4 servings). Top with small amount of nondairy topping just before serving.

You are now ready to serve this special meal. Pour the water in the soup, add the crouton, and enjoy your soup à l'oignon. Next comes salade verte with vinaigrette dressing. Then dish out the chicken, along with the sauce, onions, and potatoes on the same plate. You can group the onions on one side and the potatoes on the other side of the chicken in an artful manner. Put a low-calorie whipped topping on the chocolate mousse, add the foamed milk and boiling water to make cappucino, and you have a wonderful meal for company.

Kitchen Cleanup as Follows:

Put the one extra portion of coq au vin in the refrigerator for later freezing. Unplug the frying pan, tip over the edge, and discard any waste right into your sink. Wash the frying pan and dry it with a paper towel. Wash the serving spoon, knife, fork, and blender and leave them out.

Are you surprised? Did you doubt that we were serious? We hope we've convinced you and you'll want to have somebody for dinner.

Now that you have a good idea of what we have in mind, we'd like to give you some recipes for the rest of the week and then briefly discuss some broad, general cooking methods. Remember that basically you are taking the meat or poultry, perhaps shaking on a little flour to give the sauce heft, adding vegetables or fruits and some sort of a liquid to make a sauce, and seasoning. Cooking meat or poultry with almost innumerable combinations of the above at a slow simmer covered for forty-five minutes or so will produce a soft, tender, delectable dish.

Other Main Dishes for the First Week

CHICKEN CACCIATORE

1. Shake two chicken pieces in a paper or plastic bag with 1 heaping tablespoon of flour and 1/2 teaspoon of pepper (estimate measurements after the first time).

2. Spray electric skillet with vegetable cooking spray.

3. Turn skillet to 250° and brown chicken for a few moments.

4. Add one small 16-oz. can stewed tomatoes. Add 1/4 cup water.

5. Sprinkle on 1/2 teaspoon oregano, 1/2 teaspoon onion powder, and 1/2 teaspoon garlic powder (estimate measurements after the first time).

6. Let come to a boil; turn down to simmer, cover, and cook a total of 40 minutes or until fork-tender.

CURRIED CHICKEN

1. Shake 2 chicken pieces in a paper or plastic bag with 1 heaping tablespoon of flour, 1 teaspoon of chili powder, 1/2 teaspoon of curry, and a few dashes of pepper (estimate measurements after the first time).

2. Spray an electric skillet with vegetable cooking spray.

3. Turn skillet to 250° and brown chicken lightly for a few moments.

, 15–22 minutes; corn on the cob, 16–20 minutes; frozen
19–22 minutes; frozen green beans, 24–26 minutes; frozen
17 minutes; fish filets, 7–10 minutes; rice, long grain, with
rice and one cup water in bowl placed on steaming rack with
eneath, 26–30 minutes; sweet potatoes or carrots, 25 minutes;
gus, 10 minutes; summer squash, 7 minutes; carrots, 20 min-
You can even steam chicken—sprinkle on paprika, oregano,
c and onion powder—try 25 minutes.

or hors d'oeuvres, how about French crudités, a dish with sliced
cchini with the skin on, cucumber with the skin, some sardines,
d some canned sliced beets? This is a wonderful dish for guests,
ho can help themselves, using small paper plates. You can make a
nice dip using yogurt and dill powder. Sprinkle in to taste.

For other green salads, iceberg lettuce keeps a long time. Make
hearts of lettuce. Cut the lettuce into wedges. Use the same salad
dressing or commercial Italian without sugar in it.

Eat other salad vegetables without too much fuss. For instance,
buy unwaxed cucumbers, wash them off, and eat them with the peel.
Don't buy a vegetable that looks sandy or is packaged in such a way
that there will be a lot of work to get it ready to eat.

Here's a way to handle pasta: Spaghetti or other pastas should be
boiled in the electric frying pan. There is a wooden pasta remover
especially made for spaghetti. This inexpensive tool will allow you to
remove the spaghetti from the water without burning yourself.

As regards desserts, the mousse recipe we gave you can be varied
by just changing the low-calorie pudding mix. It's a special treat and
full of calcium and high-quality protein and is low in fat. Otherwise,
stick to fresh fruit or canned fruits in unsweetened syrup or calorie-
controlled frozen pops or something similar. One thing is certain—
don't eat junk. Nothing loaded with table sugar, butter, or cream is
advisable. Don't consider those things special treats any longer.

Snacks

We all love to snack. We recommend skim milk, fruit, or that
greatest of all snacks, popcorn. Popcorn is high in fiber, low in calo-

4. Add 1½ cups hot water broth and seasoning, chicken fla

5. Let come to a boil; turn dov total of 40 minutes or until fork-ten

MEATBALLS DEL

1. Form ½ pound extra-lean ground c using water to moisten or about 2 tablespoo

2. Add ½ teaspoon onion powder, ½ tea and 1 pinch thyme (estimate measurements afte

3. Spray a skillet with vegetable cooking spray.

4. Brown the meatballs on all sides at 250°–300°.

5. Push the meatballs to the edge of the skillet, down, and wipe away any extra fat with a wad of pape.

6. Cover and cook at 200° for about 10 minutes, then plain spaghetti sauce, if desired, and simmer 10 minutes lo

FISH FOR A KING

1. Put a rack and a small amount of water in the electric fryii. pan or an electric wok.

2. Place washed vegetables, such as sweet potato and broccoli, on the rack and steam for 18 minutes.

3. Add codfish or other firm fish, 2 pieces, sprinkled with paprika, parsley flakes, and a little lemon juice, and steam 7 minutes more.

You can vary the spices and liquids yourself, once you have the basic idea of how to set up a meal without doing a lot of preliminary chopping, mixing, measuring, and mincing, and using one electric frying pan.

For an easy way with vegetables, use the second electric frying pan or an electric wok with a steaming rack in it. Put in enough water so that it lies just below the rack. The only precaution is to lift the cover in such a way that the steam escapes away from you.

Approximate and sample steaming times: broccoli, 24–26 minutes;

ries. Make popcorn using regular kernels (not gourmet) in a hot-air popper. A combination of garlic powder and onion powder turns popcorn into a luscious dish in which you'll never miss the butter or salt. Empty the popcorn into a paper bag, put in the spices and shake.

We've come to the end of our cooking hints section. You can see that we've given you ideas on which to build and simple cooking techniques that will result in gourmet meals, delicious sauces, and combinations of vegetables that are nutritious and satisfying. You really can't be bothered too much with recipes, especially complicated recipes. You have to think about how things taste, learn to put ingredients together, and commit yourself to cooking a great meal without making a lot of work either at the time of cooking or at cleanup time. If at the end of a meal you have a pile of dishes and pots and pans, you simply won't do that every night. If you learn to cook in the way we've told you, you'll have fun and surprise yourself and your friends.

You can see that once you begin thinking in the right direction, the possibilities are endless. So get up your courage and turn yourself into an instant gourmet. Keep notes on what turns out right, and if something isn't up to your idea of perfection, remember, using our techniques, it will still be nutritious and low in saturated fats.

If you dislike, or cannot tolerate, broccoli, what food *can* you talk about with your friends? Use sweet potatoes as your miracle food (high in vitamins A and C, fiber, and a good starch that doesn't bounce your blood sugar around). The real miracle is good nutrition. You can vary any individual food on the Healthy Core diet.

We hope this chapter, as with others in this book, opens up a whole new way of life for you. Plenty of good food is essential for "living well."

5

Exercise

FINDING THE ATHLETE INSIDE YOU

Can we be serious? Perhaps you haven't walked more than a block or two in years. You are a product of millions of years of roaming, hunting ancestors that survived by physical activity. Athleticism is as much a part of your inheritance as a human being as is your mental ability. All you have to do to let out the athlete buried inside of you is to claim that inheritance. Find the will and the courage to grasp what is rightfully yours. With rare exceptions, your performance can improve in a training program, just as any other athlete's performance improves. You can attain fitness based on your own individual needs and abilities.

But, you may be thinking, what *is* fitness, anyway? What can I *expect* from being fit? And why bother?

Being fit means that your body has sufficient flexibility, muscle strength, and heart and lung power to perform the tasks you need to do to "live well."

Now here's what to expect:

- Heart, lungs, and blood vessels that work better
- Blood pressure lowered

- Possibly less chance of developing heart disease, and less chance of pulmonary infections that develop in people who are sedentary
- Experience less tension and stress
- Better control over body fat
- Fewer problems with deterioration of bones and joints
- A day-to-day feeling of well-being, physical as well as mental
- Feeling happier
- Feeling better about your body
- More energy at the end of the day
- Energy and ability to do the things you'd given up—you thought —forever
- A natural high from exercise, instead of from cigarettes, alcohol, or drugs
- A better sex life

You might be thinking, "Can I really expect that?" Well, why not try and see for yourself? A great new world is about to open up for you as you experience the joy of moving your body once again. Here's exactly how to do it: step-by-step instructions to becoming an athlete. Let's work together to bring out that athlete.

CARDIOPULMONARY CONDITIONING

Cardiopulmonary conditioning results in the most efficient heart, lungs, and blood vessels possible for you. Each of us has a "maximum heart rate" (hereafter referred to as MAX). This is the upper limit of how fast our hearts can beat from doing vigorous activity. Predicted MAX is determined by age and not training. MAX is calculated by subtracting your age from the number 220. Therefore, a fifty-five-year-old man has a predicted MAX of 165 beats per minute. So, you might ask, if it's all predetermined, why bother training? After all, predicted MAX drops with age and the greatest athlete cannot change it. But here's what *can* change: how fast and hard your heart will have to beat to do various tasks. If walking down the street makes your heart approach your MAX, then you will be struggling for breath and can do no more. With the training we'll describe, however, you might be able to walk down five streets and still never approach MAX. *That's* what we're going to try to achieve. The kind of training that will result in your heart beating slowly and evenly during exercises and tasks that you do all day will mean that you will have more energy and the ability to go longer and further in your own daily activities. Your heart will not have to beat furiously to do a minor task. Can you imagine what a difference that will make in your life? What you will gain can be called *endurance*. If now you have to huff and puff and stop after climbing only a few stairs, or after walking only half a block, with training you might be able to do that with a very moderate amount of effort. Endurance can be the difference between barely getting your activities of daily living accomplished and having enough energy at the end of the day to enjoy yourself, to socialize, to go to the movies, to go shopping and carry your own bundles, to drive your car, or to go for a walk with your mate or a friend. It can mean not sitting around all day only doing sedentary activities, and it can mean increased ability to have sex and enjoy it more. Because your heart and lungs will be stronger and more efficient, oxygen will be delivered throughout your body with less work. New and expanded blood vessels may form in exercised muscles, providing roadways to carry oxygen. Blood vessels may become more pliable and blood pressure may fall to more normal limits. Fatigue, that terrible enemy of the pulmonary patient, can *decrease!*

To attain cardiopulmonary conditioning, you need your doctor's permission, help, and guidance. When not contraindicated, exercise testing is a valuable tool to help assess your pulmonary function and to help in designing your exercise program. Here's how you can start to attain cardiopulmonary conditioning and begin a training program in an easy-to-follow step-by-step procedure.

Taking an Exercise Tolerance Test (Stress Test)

An exercise tolerance test is the observation and recording of an individual's cardiopulmonary responses during increasing levels of physical work. A stress test is usually done to rule out heart disease. In your case you also need a measurement of your lungs' ability to take up and utilize oxygen. In a stress test, with a doctor in the room, you walk on a treadmill or ride a special bicycle called an ergometer while your heart waves and rate are continuously monitored. In addition, there are several ways in which your blood oxygen can be measured. You might wear a small nonpainful clip on your ear containing a sensing device. This device will constantly read the amount of oxygen in your blood. This is called ear oximetry. A second method is to have your oxygen and other blood gases measured by drawing blood from an artery before, during, and immediately after the exercise test. A third method is to measure your body's actual uptake of oxygen by a mouthpiece attached to a small computer. This is called a metabolic measurement cart. We feel that it is important for the pulmonary patient to have this additional measurement during an exercise test. You may have no visible signs of heart disease, but if your blood oxygen falls off instead of rising as it should as the energy and oxygen demands of the test increase, then you might do better exercising with portable oxygen. In fact, your doctor may want to do two exercise tolerance tests, one with and one without oxygen, to see whether your endurance can increase with the use of oxygen, and this test may be repeated again at a later date to check on your improvement. The pulmonary laboratory at the nearest medical center may be the best place for you to take your exercise tolerance test. *Remember,* measurement of oxygen and blood gases is very important.

Here are some facts to help take the stress out of your stress test. Don't eat for at least two hours before getting your test. The preceding meal should be a light one, low in fat. Eliminate all sources of caffeine, including coffee, tea, and caffeinated beverages such as colas for at least twelve to twenty-four hours prior to the test. Unless otherwise advised, take all your medications as usual. Wear jogging shoes or sneakers (or the best walking shoes that you have); don't bring slippers! Men: bring gym shorts, Bermuda shorts, or a pair of loose-fitting light trousers. Women: wear a bra, a loose-fitting short-sleeved blouse that buttons in the front, and slacks, shorts, or even pajama bottoms. Don't wear one-piece undergarments or panty hose. Go through the test calmly and with a sense of adventure. There will be a doctor in the room with you. Insist on a trial walk on the treadmill before starting a treadmill test. If you feel light-headed, have chest pains, get anxious, and want to call the test off at any time, that's your option. Just say so. You will start off by moving very slowly on the treadmill and measurements will be taken constantly. The treadmill will not go faster or be elevated in any way until the doctor is assured that you are doing well and can handle a slightly harder task, and then the workload is increased very gently and gradually. Talk to the doctor giving you the test and get a feeling of confidence in him. Before the test, if you are a man, your chest will be shaved in order to allow placement of the electrocardiogram electrodes. After the completion of the walking part of the test, you will lie down. Measurements will continue as your heart and lungs return to a resting state. It would be best if someone would go to the test with you in case you are exceptionally tired at the completion. Look at stress testing as an exciting experience; have courage and don't be afraid. This is the first step toward becoming an athlete!

The Exercise Prescription

The exercise tolerance test has told your doctor the capabilities of your heart, lungs, and muscles and whether you need portable oxygen during your training program. It also can tell him the safe heart rate range over which you can train. Do you remember the maximum heart rate we described earlier, which averages 220 beats per minute *minus* your age? To produce cardiopulmonary efficiency, you must train at a rate as close as possible to 70 to 85 percent of your maximum heart rate (MAX). At first, you may not be able to achieve that and may have to begin at 60 percent. You should, however, work toward it. This is a heart rate range which will produce maximal cardiopulmonary benefits and the kind of endurance and yes—athleticism—that we described. This heart rate range as prescribed by your doctor is called the training sensitive zone (hereafter referred to as TSZ). A typical TSZ for an average healthy fifty-five-year-old man would be as follows: MAX 220 − 55 = 165 and 70% of 165 = 115; 85% of 165 = 140. Therefore, the TSZ for an average person fifty-five years of age is 115 to 140 beats per minute. Your training zone may be different because of the limitations of pulmonary disease. No matter. Unless your doctor disapproves of the TSZ concept for you, don't leave the office without this exercise heart range. This is the range that is safe for you. You will use your TSZ once you get used to it, not only during exercise but during all of your activities. You won't have to be afraid anymore. You will know that you are within a safe pulse range. You will use your TSZ when walking, having sex, going to the movies, going shopping, fishing, climbing up a hill, etc. This is your safe heart rate zone. It can change, because people change. It can go up or down. But you need your TSZ as a guide to begin this program. You also need the rest of the exercise prescription. How long should you keep your heart in the TSZ? How often? Should you walk or ride a stationary bicycle? Should you use supplemental oxygen? If so, how much? These are all important questions for you. Even if you haven't had a stress test, get exact answers. For most people, we suggest walking. Show your doctor the walk program. Ask if you can use it and ask him to check the appropriate starting level that's right for you. The most likely choice will be Level 1. You now have your exercise prescription. Becoming an athlete is within your grasp. Let's get to work! Don't overdo, but don't be worried by a few minor aches. Get your doctor's support and get working!

SUGGESTED TRAINING PROGRAM

The components in the pulmonary exercise program for cardiopulmonary conditioning are: stretching-flexibility warm-up, stretching-flexibility exercises, warm-up phase, TSZ time, cool-down phase, and post-cool-down flexibility and stretching. Let us explain in detail. Let us say, first off, that if there is a group exercise program in your area, perhaps at the YMCA, perhaps designed for the cardiac patient and regulated by pulse and exercise time, try to get into it. You will be able to exercise under supervision. This will be helpful, especially to get going. Perhaps there is a cardiac rehabilitation program at your local hospital. The level at which you function might be different, but the principles are the same. See if you can entice them to let you into it. If you are really lucky, there might even be a pulmonary rehabilitation program. Once *you* get going, perhaps you can get a community pulmonary exercise program started!

Before we begin explaining the components of your training program in detail, here are a few exercise how-to's. How to take your pulse:

Place the tips of your fingers on the thumb side of your wrist. Having found your pulse, it is important to count accurately. You are only going to count for 10 seconds and multiply by 6, and therefore, accuracy is essential. If you are off by one beat, then your minute reading will be in error by six beats. You should take your pulse while moving, but if you can't, just try moving in place and take your pulse right away. Know your 10-second heart rate zone and practice. To get your 10-second pulse zone, divide the upper and lower limits of your TSZ by 6: TSZ of 115–140 = 10-second zone of 19–23. If you absolutely can't get your pulse at the wrist, buy an inexpensive stethoscope at a surgical supply store. Tape it to your chest under your left nipple, or wherever your heart sounds the loudest, put it in your ears when you are ready, and count your heartbeat. The times to take your pulse are as follows:

1. Take a resting pulse in the morning before you get out of bed. Hopefully, your resting pulse will decrease as fitness improves. If your resting pulse drops from 80 to 70, this means there are 10 fewer beats per minute; there will be 600 fewer beats required per hour; in 24 hours, 14,400 beats are "saved"—a sign of the heart's increased efficiency!

2. Take the next pulse before you begin to exercise.

3. During exercise, take your pulse every 2 minutes. Once you can exercise continuously for 15 minutes, take it every 5 minutes.

4. Take your pulse again at the end of the cool-down period.

When you walk, you should keep your body erect or lean slightly forward, your shoulders relaxed and down. Let your arms swing naturally. An exaggerated arm swing is inefficient. Step right out, gazing straight ahead. Picture an object about thirty feet away. Do not shuffle. Increase your stride length to increase efficiency. If you would like to walk faster, raise the arms to about waist height and bend at the elbows and make a gentle opposing swinging action of the arms as you swivel your hips slightly. This will increase your stride length and the speed at which you can move. Remember, most of us get places by walking, not jogging or running. Always try to go longer, not necessarily faster. Keep to the lower level of your TSZ as much as possible. Don't go above your TSZ and never go to MAX except under laboratory conditions.

The ideal temperature for exercising outdoors is between 40° and 60° F. The windchill factor on colder days must be taken into account. Rapid walking will cause a tenfold increase in heat production over that associated with the resting state. Therefore, you can dress quite lightly and just risk being a little cold at the start. On the other hand, do not go far afield on a cold day. The sun may disappear or the wind may come up, affecting the windchill factor and lowering the temperature drastically (see the Windchill Chart in Chap. 3). When you exercise, sweating is a natural product of a good exercise workout. The body produces heat, as we just described. Sweating cools the body, but it can also freeze, leaving you feeling wet or damp and chilled on a freezing cold day. Therefore, when you are exercising in the winter, exercise in an area which is effectively in a circle with your home in the middle, so you can get back to your home quickly before hypothermia (excessive coolness of the body) occurs.

After exercise, get yourself into dry, warm clothing such as a turtleneck and a pair of slacks. Never take a hot shower or steam bath after exercising. Take only a lukewarm shower and then it is best to wait thirty minutes. A hand-held shower with a vibrating head is inexpensive and will feel wonderful.

You can dress yourself in layers during the cool seasons. The first layer could be long polypropylene or wool blend underwear and socks to wick away sweat. Over that, a woolen sweater and pants. If you need additional layers over that, put on another sweater made of wool or a garment made of insulating material, e.g., down or fiber fill, and then a nylon-type wind-breaking outer layer. If possible, all the upper body garments should be zipped or buttoned in such a way that they can be loosened easily when you are overheating. At night, wear reflective strip material on your clothing. Woolen mittens are warmer than gloves. Be sure to wear a hat down over your ears. For those people sensitive to cold air, put a scarf under both sides of your hat, over the nose, and under the eyes. Inexpensive cold-weather masks are available at your drugstore. Modify your own wardrobe to generally fit this category. Inexpensive sweat pants that have elasticized bottoms are very helpful as well as a zippered jacket with a hood. You might also consider an outdoor nylon running suit with a vented jacket.

When you exercise in warm weather, wear sun screens and dress lightly in running shorts and a short-sleeved top. You're an athlete, so you can dress like one! Do not exercise outside if temperatures are above 85° or humidity above 70 percent. (See the Temperature and Humidity Chart in Chap. 3.) Once again, if you keep yourself in a circle around your home base, you can always "call it off" and go home and you will not find yourself overheated. Drink fluids anytime you are thirsty—don't worry about overdoing it—you can't. Water should be cool—not ice-cold.

You will need the same great shoe as any runner or jogger. Go to the most sophisticated sporting store available. Don't worry if your physique is different from that of the other customers. Your purpose is the same. You're in the exercise crowd now. Besides, you will love your jogging shoes and will probably have to force yourself out of them for dress occasions. Check out the following: (1) Is the shoe extremely light? (2) Is there leather reinforcement on the sides of the shoe to prevent "foot drift"? (3) Is the tongue padded to prevent blistering from friction of the laces. (4) Is the toe box roomy enough to accommodate your toes so they can flex while standing, with no prominent stitchery in the toe box? (5) Does the shoe fit relatively snugly without being tight, with no feeling of discomfort from external pressures anywhere? (6) Is there a sole to provide support for your arches? (7) Is the outsole thick, yet soft enough to cushion your foot and to keep it from turning? (8) Is there a padded Achilles tendon protector? (9) Is there an ample collar, padded to reduce pressure and friction and hold your heel in place?

You've come a long way. You're suited up; you look the part; you know so many things you didn't know before. Here is the training regimen. Take it and adapt it to your own needs and abilities.

Stretching and Flexibility

These exercises stretch the muscles and tendons to increase the range of motion of the joints, thereby minimizing the number of injuries. Tight muscles may result in strains and cramps, and besides, having a supple, flexible body feels good.

Stretching routines are as important after exercises as they are before. After exercise, stretching will reduce the tightening effect that occurs as a result of vigorous movement of muscles.

Important points to remember while doing flexibility stretching exercises:

1. Stretch slowly and smoothly—*don't bounce;* bouncing can pull muscles.

2. Let the muscle stretch itself by attaining the position in which you feel a slight pulling sensation, and *hold* that position for ten to thirty seconds.

3. Breathe easily during stretching; don't hold your breath.

4. Remember, the purpose is to stretch and obtain suppleness and *not* to strain yourself.

5. *Train—don't strain!*

Stretching-flexibility warm-ups

1. Sit comfortably in a chair and make a circle with both feet simultaneously, slowly and easily, for about thirty seconds.

2. Tap your feet gently for another thirty seconds, one after the other. Go slowly; you are just warming up.

3. While sitting, extend both arms out to the side and do arm circles, five circles forward and five backward to begin.

4. Repeat steps 1, 2 and 3 twice.

While doing the above, do not slouch. Sit up and keep the spine straight.

(Fig. 19) Gastroc Stretch. Relax the upper body against the wall; bring the feet back with a straight leg until you feel a gentle ache in the back of the calves. Hold it for thirty seconds. Repeat twice.

(Fig. 20) Achilles Tendon Stretch. Walk slowly on your heels for twenty-five steps.

(Fig. 21) Quad Stretch. Lean against the wall with your arm for support and lift your leg behind you. Hold for ten seconds. Bring the knee back until you feel an ache in the thigh area. Release; change legs. Do each side at least three times.

(Fig. 22) Side Stretch. Stand comfortably, legs shoulder-width apart. Raise your left hand overhead and lean to the right without moving your feet. Hold for ten seconds. Repeat each side at least twice.

(Fig. 23) Total Body Stretch. (A) Stand with the legs shoulder-width apart and the back straight, arms up. Reach for the sky. (B) Rise on the toes and hold for ten seconds. (C) With a slightly bent knee, bend over and hang for ten seconds. Do once.

The Warm-up

To warm up, walk, gradually increasing the speed, to bring your pulse rate to just below your TSZ over a seven-minute period. Do not enter your TSZ. This allows your cardiopulmonary system and muscles to adjust *gradually* to increasing energy and oxygen requirements and prevents early burnout, pain, and exhaustion. *Do not skip the warm-up!* You may lengthen it, but do not shorten it.

Training-Sensitive-Zone Time

This is the most important component of your training regimen. During your TSZ time, you increase your effort and bring your heart rate into the prescribed range. It's increasing your TSZ duration that leads to endurance. Stretching-flexibility and warm-up are all appetizers. *This* is your main course! Your ultimate goal is to keep your pulse in the TSZ for twenty to thirty minutes three times a week (four times is even better!) on nonconsecutive days. It may take many weeks or months to accomplish this. Consider this a long-term, lifetime project. Increase your TSZ time very gradually. We have given you a suggested training table.

On alternate days do less strenuous activities. When exercising in your TSZ, exercise by pulse and time. Do *not* try to cover a preset distance. By this we mean: Do not try to complete the same distance every training day. Factors such as wind, humidity, pollution, and pollen count change the amount of effort required. Sometimes you will have to walk slowly or your pulse will be too rapid.

Exercising by time and pulse allows for these changing conditions and gives you flexibility. You can vary your "fit trail" from somewhat hilly terrain to a walk in the mall. In fact, your local mall is a great place to exercise in bad weather.

If your TSZ time is fifteen minutes or more, take your pulse every five minutes. If your TSZ time is less than fifteen minutes, take your pulse every three minutes.

Self-evaluation in the TSZ is important. In addition to pulse taking, learn to notice how you are feeling and how you are breathing.

You should be breathing deeply, but not be "hungry" for air. You should be working hard, but exertion should not be severe. If you can't talk, you're overdoing. Test this even if you have to talk to yourself. Anxiety, nervousness, nausea, light-headedness, and chest pain are all signs that you should slow down. Do not stop abruptly unless you can't avoid it. (See "Cool-Down" below.) When you finish exercising in your TSZ, you should feel happy, not tense, and you should be looking forward to your next "TSZ encounter."

If you absolutely need an additional aid to keep your pulse in your TSZ, you might want to look into the purchase or use of the Exersentry electronic heart rate monitor made by Respironics, Inc., available at athletic or surgical supply stores. This small sensing device attaches to the chest and reads out your heart rate constantly. The lower and upper limits of your TSZ are then dialed in.

If you go above your TSZ, a gentle alarm will sound and continue sounding until you have slowed down and your heart rate has fallen back to a safe range.

Cool-down

The purpose of the cool-down is to allow the heart, lungs, and muscles to recover gradually. It also gives a chance for the large pool of blood that is now in the extremities to be redistributed back to the central part of the body. In the cool-down you simply return to the warm-up walk rate. Cool down by walking for approximately five minutes. Remember to *keep moving* and do not stop! Blood pooling can cause fainting. At the completion of the cool-down, take your pulse. It should be below 120 or back to resting level. If not, decrease your TSZ time by going back one level on your training sheet.

Post-cool-down Stretching Flexibility

This relieves the increased contraction of muscles which occurs with strenuous exercise, decreases the number of postexercise aches and pains, and contributes further to overall suppleness and flexibility. Repeat *all* the stretching-flexibility exercises at this point.

If your physician doesn't wish to give you a TSZ, you can still follow all the previously described principles of exercise. Try to at least obtain an upper safe heart rate limit.

A Twelve-Minute Test

Now that you understand the basics of a training program, why not take a twelve-minute walk test and record the results? Simply put, this is the distance you can walk in twelve minutes—comfortably and with no strain. Pick a safe walkway, preferably around your house. You don't need to continue walking for the full twelve minutes. You may stop any time you want. In fact, be sure there are plenty of chairs and stop areas along your walkway. Just walk comfortably, and at the end of twelve minutes, record the approximate distance. Here are examples: 550 yards; five times around the living room; one time the length of the mall. Record the results. You will want to repeat the twelve-minute walk test regularly to check your progress. During the test, take your pulse now and again to make sure you're not out of a safe range. You may take the test with or without oxygen. Be sure to record that information. Don't overdo during this test. This is *not* a maximum stress test!

The Exercise Diary

Your progress may astound you. Each time you exercise, you should make an entry in your exercise diary. Please look carefully at it now as we explain each column. Take a large index card or other firm piece of paper which can comfortably fit in your pocket, and copy the columns onto it. At the top, write your TSZ and your ten-second TSZ. If these change, go to a new diary card. The first column, of course, is the date. The next column is your morning resting pulse. Take this *before* you get out of bed. Hopefully, your pulse rate will eventually drop as your cardiopulmonary efficiency increases. You will find some variation in your pulse from day to day. Learn what is acceptable regarding variation in pulse for you and what may be your relapse rate. (See Chap. 3.) The next column is for recording your pulse just prior to any exercise activity, including stretching and flexibility. There are then three columns in which to record

EXERCISE DIARY

Training Sensitive Zone _____

10-second TSZ _____

DATE	A.M. RESTING PULSE	PRE-EXER. PULSE	EXER. PULSE (1)	EXER. PULSE (2)	EXER. PULSE (3)	POST-EXER. PULSE (minutes) 3 5	DURATION TIME AT TRAINING ZONE (total exercise time)	COMMENTS

subsequent pulses during exercise. The next column is to record your pulse at three and five minutes after exercise is completed. Next, record your total duration time of exercise and then your TSZ time. You will want to see those figures going up. Remember, even an increase of thirty seconds in TSZ time could be a triumph. The last column is for comments, e.g., "easy day" or "easily winded today". Be sure to record any of the danger signals already discussed, should they occur.

You should show the diary to your doctor regularly, and, in fact, if you don't see him very often, ask if you might mail your results in to him. If you are sending the original cards, remember to ask that he return them to you after checking to see that there are no untoward signs or symptoms being recorded by you. Solicit your doctor's cooperation here. You need his help and guidance.

Walk Program

Do *not* progress to the next level until you have successfully completed a level at least six times. After two weeks on this program, you can tell all your friends that you "work out" regularly!

STARTER LEVEL

	Warm up	Training-Target TSZ in Minutes	Cool Down	Total Time
LEVEL 1	Walk slowly 7 min.	Then walk briskly 3 min.	Then walk slowly 5 min.	15 min.

YOU MAY INCREASE YOUR TSZ TIME BY 1 MINUTE INSTEAD OF 2 (OR 30 SEC. INSTEAD OF 1 MIN.!)

	Warm up	Training-Target TSZ in Minutes	Cool Down	Total Time
LEVEL 2	Walk slowly 7 min.	Walk briskly 5 min.	Walk slowly 5 min.	17 min.

INTERMEDIATE LEVEL

	Warm up	Training-Target TSZ in Minutes	Cool Down	Total Time
LEVEL 3	Walk slowly 7 min.	Walk briskly 7 min.	Walk slowly 5 min.	19 min.
LEVEL 4	Walk slowly 7 min.	Walk briskly 9 min.	Walk slowly 5 min.	21 min.

	Warm Up	Training-Target TSZ in Minutes	Cool Down	Total Time
BRONZE LEVEL				
LEVEL 5	Walk slowly 7 min.	Walk briskly 11 min.	Walk slowly 5 min.	23 min.
LEVEL 6	Walk slowly 7 min.	Walk briskly 13 min.	Walk slowly 5 min.	25 min.
LEVEL 7	Walk slowly 7 min.	Walk briskly 15 min.	Walk slowly 5 min.	27 min.
LEVEL 8	Walk slowly 7 min.	Walk briskly 17 min.	Walk slowly 5 min.	29 min.

AWARD YOURSELF THE BRONZE MEDAL UPON COMPLETION OF THE ABOVE!

SILVER LEVEL				
LEVEL 9	Walk slowly 5 min.	Walk briskly 23 min.	Walk slowly 5 min.	33 min.
LEVEL 10	Walk slowly 5 min.	Walk briskly 26 min.	Walk slowly 5 min.	36 min.
LEVEL 11	Walk slowly 5 min.	Walk briskly 28 min.	Walk slowly 5 min.	38 min.

AWARD YOURSELF THE SILVER MEDAL UPON COMPLETION OF THE ABOVE!

GOLD LEVEL				
LEVEL 12	Walk slowly 5 min.	Walk briskly 30 min.	Walk slowly 5 min.	40 min.

GIVE YOURSELF THE GOLD!

If you can't go outdoors, go to your local mall. At home, move your arms and legs to music, or walk around your living room. Ride a stationary bicycle or jump rope *without* a rope by a loping action with one foot in front of the other. Always follow your training schedule. Always use the same format of stretching, warm-up time, TSZ time, and cool-down. And, last but not least, get yourself one of those inexpensive, sporty black plastic LCD watches with a stop-watch feature. And how about a waist-held miniature radio or tape deck with earphones?

Bodybuilding and Weight Training

Yes! You can do it! You want to have good general upper and lower body strength. You want a good strong back, and for that you need strong abdominal muscles. You want to be able to open up a jar that's stuck, and to carry a package. You want not only cardiopulmonary conditioning, you want to attain good total body strength and flexibility. The good athlete is an all-around person. To "live well" with COPD, you must be restricted as little as possible from enjoying the ordinary activities of daily living that are available to you. You're not going to become a professional weight lifter, but weight training—that is, lifting light weights—can make an enormous difference in your everyday life. A good time to do weight training is directly after completing the cardiopulmonary training program for the day. Your muscles will be supple and still ready for action, and you will have a glorious feeling following your walk or after riding your bicycle.

To do weight training, begin with 1-pound weights. Try 1-pound cans of food as the simplest way to start weight lifting. When you have determined that 1-pound weights feel extremely light to you, switch to 3-pound weights which are easy to purchase. Try six repetitions to begin with for each of the following exercises and call this one set. Try to build up the number of repetitions to twelve. Eventually you can build up the number of sets. Set reasonable goals. Back off if your muscles become sore—it's not necessary. If there is a burning sensation in your muscles, they are exercising vigorously. Once you feel the burn, that's enough of that exercise for the day. Please see illustrations:

Sit back in the chair in which you did your stretching warm-ups. Ideally, it should have no arms. Try to do each exercise six times to start.

Half a Head Roll: Gently roll the head from side to side. Roll the head to the right, then back to the left. Rolling the head in both directions is one repetition.

Shoulder Roll: Rotate the shoulders gently forward six times and gently backward six times.

Small Forward Arm Row: With the arms extended, rotate the arms six times in a small circle forward.

Large Forward Arm Row: With the arms extended, rotate the arms six times in a large circle forward.

Large Backward Arm Roll: Rotate the arms six times using a backward motion with the arms held extended.

Open Shoulder Flexibility: Put the right hand behind the head and try to grasp your fingers with the left hand behind the back. Now switch off and put the left hand behind the back and try to grasp the fingers of the right hand. This exercise can be done three times instead of six. It keeps the shoulder joints open. Women need open shoulders to do such basic tasks as fastening their bra. Men need it to pull up their pants. (Fig. 24)

Forward Lift with Weights: Pick up a 1-pound weight in each hand. Proper breathing technique is now essential. Inhale *prior* to lifting the weight. Exhale *as the weight is being lifted.* Lift the weights to shoulder height in front of you. Slowly bring your arms back to your sides. (Fig. 25)

Sideward Lift with Weights: Take a breath. As you are exhaling, slowly bring the arms sideward to shoulder level and then back down slowly. (Fig. 26)

Backward Lift: Bring your arms gently backward at no more than a thirty-degree angle behind your body and return slowly. Use the same proper breathing techniques. (Fig. 27)

Forward Row: Simulate a rowing action. Do this slowly and remember to use the proper breathing techniques. (Fig. 28)

Biceps Curls: Start with arms at your sides, then contract the elbows and bring the weights to your shoulders. (Fig. 29)

Now put your weights aside.

Abdominal Muscle Contractions: Sit comfortably in a chair. Contract your abdominal muscles. Bring your belly in.

PC Contraction: "PC" stands for "pubococcygeal muscle." This is

24. Open Shoulder Flexibility.
25. Forward Lift.
26. Sideward Lift.

the muscle that contracts during sexual activity. Better development will heighten sexual sensation and control. This part of your body should be as well conditioned as the rest of you. Contract the muscle by making the same motion as you would to stop the flow of urine.

Knee to Chest: Bring your knee to your chest, clasp your hands

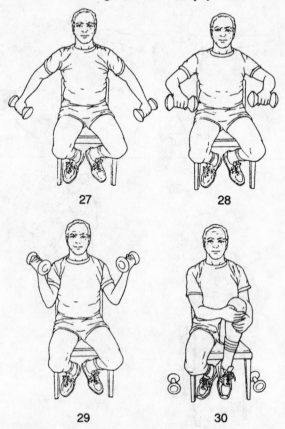

27. Backward Lift.
28. Forward Row.
29. Biceps Curls.
30. Knee to Chest.

around them. Keep your back straight and your foot pointed. Try to touch your knee to your chest for about two seconds. (Fig. 30)

Ankle Flex: Rest heels on ground. Flex the feet slowly forward and backward.

Ankle Circles: Make slow circles to right and then to left. You may rest your heels gently on the ground.

Respiratory Muscle Training

Sit still and increase your respiratory muscle power! This is a new exercise concept. You can sit still, use the device we are about to describe, and increase your respiratory-muscle endurance. Just as all your other muscles have come into disuse from being sedentary, so the muscles that control the vital movement of your lungs as you breathe have become weak from disuse and lack of exercise. As the settings on the inspiratory muscle trainer increase, the air hole diameter decreases, thus "exercising" your inspiratory muscles by making them work harder to inspire the same amount of air.

We recommend that your physician consider your using the P-flex inspiratory muscle trainer (prescription necessary). This is a small, plastic whistlelike device made by the HealthScan Company. (Fig. 31) It is very inexpensive. It's also convenient and practical for use at home. Enclosed in the trainer's package are complete instructions for an exercise program for your inspiratory muscles. In a recent study with a group of patients who used the trainer and a group who used a sham device, there was marked improvement in maximum work rate and respiratory muscle endurance in the group that used the trainer. The patients who used the sham device showed no improvement. All you do is sit quietly breathing through your P-flex and your respiratory muscles will grow stronger. A nose clip will ensure that all your air comes in through the trainer. How about performing this part of your exercise program while watching TV or reading?

You need your doctor's permission, cooperation, and advice. Read the brochure enclosed in the inspiratory muscle trainer *carefully.*

Begin with fifteen minutes daily.

Try to achieve thirty minutes a day.

When you use the muscle trainer, your respiratory rate and pulse *should not go up.* They should either remain *the same or go down.* If your respiratory rate or pulse is rising, you are using too high a setting.

Here is a sample way used in studies with the respiratory muscle

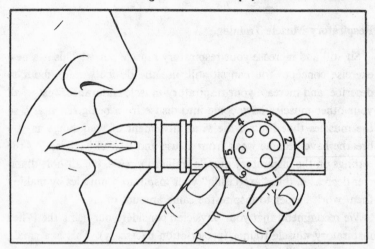

(**Fig. 31**) The P-flex Inspiratory Muscle Trainer. Sit still and increase your respiratory muscle power.

trainer to determine whether it is safe for you to go to a higher setting:

1. Use setting number 1 until you can breathe comfortably for thirty minutes and your respiratory rate and pulse are not rising. Do this for a *minimum* of one week. Note your respiratory rate and pulse while breathing on number 1.

2. Increase the respiratory rate setting to number 2. Breathe for ten to 15 minutes. Are you breathing comfortably? Is your respiratory rate and pulse *the same or lower?* If so, report this to your doctor and ask his permission to use the second setting.

3. Use the second setting for a *minimum* of one week until you are breathing comfortably for thirty minutes. Note your respiratory rate and pulse while on that setting.

4. Increase the setting to number 3. Over a ten-minute period of time, note your respiratory rate and pulse. If they are *the same or going down,* and if you feel comfortable, notify your doctor and ask his permission to increase the setting by one number.

5. Continue the use of the trainer in this manner with your doctor's permission until you reach the highest number tolerable for you. Continue to use that setting indefinitely, working your way slowly up to thirty minutes a day.

6. When you move up to a higher setting, you may be able to breathe comfortably, but only for five to ten minutes daily. Therefore, at that higher setting, gradually increase your time back up to thirty minutes.

7. If you are ill and unable to use the trainer for some period of time, go back at least one setting.

8. Be sure to note the care and washing instructions in the pamphlet.

We have come to the end of our chapter on exercise. If you've come along with us, then you've learned a great deal. Ideally you've been through a stress test and obtained a TSZ. Occasionally your doctor may not feel a stress test is appropriate. He may fix a TSZ for you based on his knowledge of you as his patient. You've taken a twelve-minute walk to sample your progress. You've had the experience of going to an athletic store and buying jogging shoes and weights. You're beginning to do things that the rest of the world is doing. When you open up a magazine, you'll understand what is meant by warm-ups, cool-downs, and TSZ or, as it's sometimes called, exercise heart range. You should buy runners' magazines and read them—why not? Buy other books on walking and cardiovascular fitness, because cardiovascular fitness treats more than the heart. It treats the whole person. You should also continue to expand your training in calisthenics. Do simple exercises which will not hurt your back or joints. Continue to lift light weights, perhaps increasing to 5 pounds in time. Watch your strength and endurance improve! This is your ultimate goal. You cannot become a competitive athlete, but you can become an all-around stronger person and be able to live a full day filled with a wide range of activities that include taking care of yourself, exercising, eating right, relaxing, enjoying recreational activities, and having fulfilling sex.

Keep reading about exercise; keep trying. Remember, this is a lifelong program. Think about it in terms of months and years, not days or weeks. You will notice improvement. A small improvement is a lot. Don't get discouraged. Ask questions, and seek advice when you need it. Don't let anything deter you from keeping up your physical activity. Keep in mind the adage "Use it or lose it!" And remember that "success breeds success."

6

Psyche

The other chapters in this book have dealt with the physical you: anatomy, physiology, nutrition, medicines, and machinery. Now we're going to talk about the psychological you: your attitudes, knowledge, emotions, and the way you behave toward others and yourself, a subject no less complicated. The physical and the emotional are irrevocably intertwined. If you don't feel well physically, it's hard to keep your spirits up. Likewise, if you're "mentally down" all the time, your physical self will also be depressed. Therefore, it's important to do some soul-searching as you read through this chapter if you don't feel happy and contented most of the time. Let's start with a brief quiz.

LEARNING ABOUT YOURSELF

1. I feel afraid a lot of the time.   Yes_____ No_____
2. Experiencing emotions, even trying to enjoy myself, makes me too short of breath, so I keep my feelings inside.   Yes_____ No_____
3. I have no one to comfort me.   Yes_____ No_____

4. I have no one to set me straight
   when I go wrong.   Yes_____ No_____
5. I get very short of breath when I
   get angry.   Yes_____ No_____
6. I avoid contact with others.   Yes_____ No_____
7. Activities outside the home don't
   interest me.   Yes_____ No_____
8. I feel worthless and dissatisfied
   with everything.   Yes_____ No_____
9. I often look back at what I've lost. Yes_____ No_____
10. Nothing can change my situation. Yes_____ No_____

This quiz reveals pertinent information about you. Before you read our explanation, do some thinking about why you answered the way you did. Make your own analysis first.

Would you say, after taking this quiz, that your situation might be described as living in a psychosocial prison? If this expression sums it up, then together we have to figure out how to get you out, make a "prison break."

Let's discuss the significance of the answers you gave in the quiz. A "yes" answer to any of the questions means that you have a problem you must deal with.

1. A "yes" answer denotes excessive fearfulness or anxiety. We all feel afraid some of the time, but most of the time is far too much. Don't settle for it—life can be much better than that. You deserve *not* to feel afraid most of the time.

2. A "yes" answer here means you are in what Dr. D. L. Dudley, Professor of Psychiatry at the University of Washington, has called the emotional straitjacket, an inability to express your emotions because you are afraid they will give you physical symptoms you can't handle such as shortness of breath and fatigue. You can't allow this either. You have to be able to cry when you must and laugh when you can.

3. Number 3 indicates social isolation, having no one who intimately cares for you and lacking a "comforter" in life. We feel that

an intimate involvement with another is essential. (We'll tell you why shortly.)

4. A "yes" denotes social isolation again, and not having the kind of intimate involvement in which you not only have a comforter but also a "concerned confronter" in life.

5. "Yes" means you're in the emotional straitjacket.

6. "Yes" means social isolation, but of another kind: lack of involvement as what we call a citizen of the world.

7. Another description of social isolation. If you answered "yes" to 3, 4, 6, and 7, then you are alone on all counts. Being alone for most people can be too difficult, too impossible, too undesirable, too sad. You owe it to yourself to correct the situation.

8. A "yes" answer denotes excessive sadness or depression, a very painful feeling. You deserve better.

9. A "yes" answer denotes depression or sadness as in question 8, coupled with a grief reaction over loss of vigor—looking backward instead of forward.

10. "Yes" means you feel that nothing, even after reading all the chapters in this book, can change your situation. Tell your doctor.

Did you get anything out of this quiz? Are these your problems? Let's add them up: (1) anxiety, (2) social isolation, (3) depression, and (4) the emotional straitjacket. What do these add up to: the psychosocial prison we mentioned earlier.

INTERPRETING WHAT YOU'VE LEARNED

Sometimes it's good to try to change the future by looking to the past. Have you ever heard the expression "You can learn a lot from an old pro"? Here's an unlikely duo: Houdini the magician and Hillel the scholar.

The great Houdini was a master of the prison escape. Houdini went into a town and offered to escape from the most secure cell in the jail. The jailers proudly showed him the cell and set down two conditions: he must be nude; he would also be handcuffed. Houdini agreed, undressed, and was locked in the cell. After being alone for a few minutes, however, he happily walked out and greeted his jailers. Houdini could do it because when inspecting the jail cell he had concealed a lock pick inside! There are three important lessons to be learned from this story. The first is that it's easy to get out of a prison if you can figure out how to pick the lock. The second is that picking the lock takes preparation and a plan. The third is that the lock pick is inside—that is, within you, within your spirit.

Are you disappointed that what Houdini did was not really magic? Of course it was magic—the magic of the resourcefulness and resiliency of the human spirit. You have that *same* gift. Use it!

Let's go back now two thousand years, when Rabbi Hillel, a famous Talmudic scholar, said, "If I am not for myself, who will be for me?" Your first obligation is to be for yourself. You must practice enlightened self-interest. You have to care about yourself and take care of yourself. Caring about yourself means eating the proper food, knowing your medications, protecting yourself from illness, and exercising regularly. It means looking out for yourself, making sure that you do things that will make you happy and content. That's what enlightened self-interest is all about. Isn't it really true? If you don't care about yourself, who will? Isn't that the way the world really is? If you want respect and dignity, you have to quietly inspire that by the way you carry yourself in life. If you act heroically you'll be treated that way. If you're babyish and dependent on other people for everything, people will look at you in that light. You have to think of yourself as unique and precious and begin to focus on all the things that *you* can do for *yourself.*

There's more to that famous quote, for Hillel also said, "If I am only for myself, what am I?" You cannot be a whole person if you are centered *only* on your own needs; nor can you expect someone else to spend his or her life centered on your needs. Give and take are necessary parts of living and loving well. You have to give to get. You must involve yourself with other people in two separate ways. The first is to become as intimately involved as possible with a single other person in a caring relationship. The kind of involvement we're talking about requires communication, reasoning, caring, and concern. These are human qualities that you possess. Make use of them. If your every thought is centered on your own needs, then you will have nothing left over for someone else, and that someone else is essential. If you have made even some parts of this book part of yourself—if you know how to eat right, exercise, take care of yourself, and if you can touch someone in any conceivably meaningful way—you definitely have something to offer to another person. You can have a genuine give-and-take relationship. If you don't have one now, find one. If you do have one, work to improve it.

The second way to involve yourself with others is as a citizen of the world—for that is what you are. You must become involved with problems and issues which go beyond your immediate concerns. Work may meet this need. If not, you should seek activities which insure your place as a citizen of the world. Are you wondering what we're talking about? You are a resident of a neighborhood, a town or city, and a state. Are there problems there? Can you help? This is your country. Can you lend a hand to a local government project? You are part of the human race with all its problems.

Can you help the environmentalists?

Can you help neighborhood children who can't read?

Can you help others break the smoking habit?

Can you call the nearest chapter of the American Lung Association and become involved? (The national office is at 1740 Broadway, New York, N.Y. 10019.)

Can you call your doctor and local community center and start a pulmonary rehabilitation program?

Can you help an organization fight poverty, disease, and starvation on the other side of the world?

And there is yet a third and final line to this quote. "If not now, when?" That's right—if not now, when? Start now. Don't give up anymore. Don't waste time grieving over the past. Start now to change things—today, this minute.

Was Hillel a man ahead of his time? We think not. More likely, the same ideas were just as true and meaningful two thousand years ago as today.

We're now going to give you proposed solutions. They are not the only solutions. Add your own, but you must come up with solutions to the problems the quiz may have disclosed. If you cannot, you must be sure to convey this to your physician.

ACTING ON YOUR DISCOVERIES: A FOUR-POINT PROGRAM

Let's methodically start to pick the lock for a prison break.

1. Start with exercise. Knowing your training sensitive zone, a safe pulse rate for you, is a valuable tool. You'll know what a healthy amount of shortness of breath feels like. You'll begin to know automatically what your body can tolerate with ease or moderate discomfort and what's too much for you. Utilize this perception of how you're doing and how hard you are working or breathing when interacting with others, when shopping, having sex, laughing, getting angry, or even feeling sad or blue. Knowing you can handle the emotion and the situation will provide an instant comfort. To know your training zone, however, you have to read the chapter on exercise carefully, go to a physician, obtain an exercise prescription, and really follow an exercise training regimen.

2. Learn all you can about your disease. Understanding your medications, knowing how to manipulate some of them with permission from your doctor, and doing your own physical self-evaluation will give back to you control over yourself. You won't be living in a fearful world, not knowing from day to day whether you will be healthy or sick. Relapses usually don't happen in a moment. They begin in a subtle way over a period of a few days. Previously, during that time, you might not have known that you were getting sick. You might not have known whether to call your doctor. Hopefully, at this point in this book you do know that, or at least you know how to work on that. Think what that can mean to you. You will not be helpless. To do this, however, you have to study, take notes, keep diaries. You have to look at yourself and give yourself time and attention each day that you may not have been used to doing before this. Your anxiety will drop when you understand your illness and how to handle it.

3. Try to get involved with a single other person and with the world as we've just described. It's time to look forward and say "I won't give up" instead of grieving over what is past and gone. Can you still enjoy the sunshine and the seasons, laugh, reason, love, get angry, want someone, need someone? If so, you can find someone. You have something to offer. Someone also needs you. Involve yourself in community activities. Give to others who are less fortunate than you are. Join social or religious organizations. Volunteer your time and talents. Do you still think you have nothing to offer to the world? Take this test: Are you reading this book? If so, could you volunteer your time to read it to somebody who is blind? If you don't take that first step toward meeting and involving yourself with others, both intimately and in the broader sense as we have described, no one will take it for you. If you do take that first step, we doubt you'll ever be sorry or want to go back to a restricted atmosphere of social isolation.

4. You've had three do's—now here's a don't. Don't give way to despair. We know you have lost a lot, but you have not lost as much as some people in this world. You have probably already had more than many millions will ever have. You can look forward. You are worthwhile. You may need help, particularly when the going gets rough and you're trying to exercise, learn about yourself, meet new people, and it all seems like an awful lot. What's wrong with getting help? Who can help? Your physician! Getting needed help is well worth your time and effort. Your alternative is to sit alone, sad, and feel sorry for yourself. In a sense, that could be easier. That's right— to give way to despair, and sit smoking and eating junk food may be easier than to face life, find something to be happy about, to laugh about, and find someone to care about. Give this a lot of thought. There's a lot at stake. Replace anxiety and despair with action.

Here is a simple final quiz for you to take:

1. I will be for myself, care about   Yes_____   No_____
myself, take care of myself, and
practice enlightened self-interest in
every way that I can, including
emotionally, socially, and vocationally.

2. I will also be for others, including   Yes_____   No_____
meeting new people, caring for
someone, touching another person
both mentally and physically, and
concerning myself with the welfare of
others and the world in general by
involvement with other people in the
human community.

3. I will start now.   Yes_____   No_____

Did you answer yes to all three questions? If so, good for you—
you've made a start. If not, be honest. Go to your physician and
discuss your feelings thoroughly and honestly.

Remember—you can break out of your prison. You have a plan,
you know how to pick the lock, and you know where the lock pick is.
You *can* succeed.

7

Sex

SEX AND THE FOUR C'S

Have you given up sex because you thought you couldn't perform? But why? To have sex you need less energy than is needed to climb up a flight of stairs slowly. What you do need is what we call the four C's: Caring, Communication, Concentration, and Commitment.

Let's examine those four ideas and you'll find that you can have great sex as a regular part of "living well" with COPD.

Caring. Caring about sex is as legitimate a concern for you as caring about any other physical function in your life. Just as your capacity to exercise can be improved by a regular program, so your sexual functioning can get better and better if you want it to and if you admit that you care about it. Think it over. It's good and right to care about sex. All forms of sex which are mutually pleasurable between you and your partner are acceptable.

Commitment. You and your partner must commit yourselves to the idea that you can have regular sexual activity. You should plan your sex, just as you plan any other important event. Don't expect it to be spontaneous. Pick a time of day when you're both fresh. If you must unexpectedly put off the act, then pick an alternate time. Both of you must be committed to the idea that sexual relations can improve your overall being. Living and loving go hand in hand. Don't make sex the last item on your list of activities for the day. Plan a special time and place that's right for both of you.

Communication. Sex is really a friendship, and no two people can be friends unless they can successfully communicate with each other. Sex is its own communication, but it cannot exist in its best form between two people who don't talk to each other. Your aim should be to talk about sex, find and understand your sexual needs, then try to meet them.

Perhaps, in the past months or years when you haven't had sex, you've lost communication with your mate or lover. It's time to get it back! Here are two good ways. This first technique is called the "holdout." Balancing compliments and criticisms, each of you should practice the "holdout" daily if need be. You begin by saying, for example:

JOHN: "I've been holding out on you."
MARY: "Yes, what is it?"

John now tells his partner something he's been keeping from her for a long time and has always wanted to tell her. The only acceptable answer from his partner at this point is "Thank you."

The "holdout" is a technique for enriching communication. It will get the air vibrating between you.

The second is called the "stop sign." When your partner doesn't really "hear" you, when he or she is giving you the same unsatisfactory or disturbing answer, hold your hand up and make a "stop sign." You both agree in advance that the talk stops and attempts at communication begin afresh.

If you've lost communication, treat each other as if you were dealing with a beautiful wild deer. Pretend you are holding out your hand, trying to feed the deer. A wrong move, and it may bolt and be gone, and you'll spend the rest of the time in the woods looking for it. Treat each other like the precious humans you are. Talk, talk, talk!

Remember you can keep talking right through having relations.

Your partner is not a magician. You have to tell him or her what is right and what is wrong, what's too light or too heavy, too fast or too slow. It's good to keep talking about sex even when sex is over. You must get your communication back. Can you do this? Can you talk to the person you love and care about and have them talk back to you? If you can, there's only one big C left—Concentration.

Concentration. Don't let your mind wander during sex. Sex does not take a great deal of physical activity; it takes *mental activity*. Concentrate on the sensations you are feeling and giving. Remember, obtaining an orgasm through your partner is your *own* responsibility. For this, you must concentrate. Don't lie there with your mind thinking of other things and expect to have a satisfying sexual experience. This act is important. Keep your mind right on the subject.

MANAGING COUGHING AND SHORTNESS OF BREATH

Sex takes preparation for the person with COPD. Pick a time of day when your chest is clear and your sputum volume is down. Use your bronchodilator and do postural drainage if necessary. If you use supplemental oxygen, you might want to turn it up about a liter with your doctor's permission. If during sex you become short of breath or have bronchospasm, don't be coy about it. Tell your partner frankly. You might want to call it off for a few moments. Put your head down and do postural drainage again. Don't get overly anxious and you'll succeed. You also must be frank. Don't expect your partner to know that at this moment your chest is constricting or that the kiss is too long and you can't breathe. Say so, and continue enjoying yourself as soon as you can.

GETTING TECHNICAL

Let's get technical by first discussing *female anatomy*. The entrance to the woman's sexual organs is surrounded by the small inner lips (labia minora). Outside are the larger lips (labia majora). Both the outer and inner lips can be pleasurably stimulated and will respond to sexual stimulation by swelling. Just below the meeting of the inner lips lies the clitoris. The clitoris is an intensely sensitive structure, analogous to the head of the penis in the male. With sexual stimulation the clitoris swells and enlarges. Below the clitoris lies the opening of the urethra. This small opening leads to the bladder for the expulsion of urine. Downward from the opening of the urethra is the vaginal opening. Inside the vagina, on the anterior wall, lies another area which can produce intense sexual pleasure. This is called the G spot. There is also a slinglike muscle which goes from anterior to posterior attached to the pubic bone in the front and the tailbone in the back. This is the pubococcygeus, or PC muscle. This muscle contracts during orgasm.

Male Anatomy. The penis is a long tube filled with three sponge-like structures which expand when filled with blood, and a narrow hollow structure which carries seminal fluid outward. When aroused, a valve closes and the spongelike structures fill with blood, causing the penis to expand, elongate, and harden and become increasingly receptive to pleasurable stimulation. Beneath and behind the penis are the two testicles enclosed in a sack called the scrotum. These produce sperm. The PC muscle, previously discussed, runs across the base of the pelvis and, when contracted, raises the penis and testicles. The prostate gland, which is interior and anterior to the anal opening, produces the vast majority of the ejaculum, and is sensitive when stimulated. The glans of the penis, or head, is exquisitely sensitive. The shaft is the next most sensitive area and the testicles less so.

Just prior to ejaculation, the testicles pull up and remain close to the body. If excitement decreases, the testicles relax again.

GETTING PHYSICAL

Let's get physical by discussing some special considerations for both women and men. The vagina secretes lubricating fluids as arousal begins. If this fluid is not adequate, try Albolene liquifying cleanser. This is a pleasant-tasting, nonodoriferous, nontoxic petroleum-jelly-like product which spreads easily over the sexual organs of both men and women.

Men might worry about impotence. Note, however, that if erection takes place at *any* time, such as in the morning, during dreams, or during self-stimulation, impotence is not a problem. It is important to note that as mid-life approaches in all men, erection and orgasm take longer to achieve and the penis may be less firm than in the first two decades of sexual life. Self-stimulation is advised to dispel any worries about impotence. In fact, self-stimulation (masturbation) is advised on a regular basis if you haven't had sex in a long time. A man can learn things about himself and show these things to his partner.

Some women tend to worry about not having an orgasm. Once again, self-stimulation can come to the rescue! If you're comfortable with it, regular self-stimulation can help to find those magic spots so that you can then communicate their locations and the kind of touch it takes for effective stimulation to your partner. Self-stimulation can be practiced together or separately with the knowledge of each partner. One thing is certain—the idea that self-stimulation is bad for you is long gone.

It is totally unnecessary and not even desirable for partners to achieve orgasm at the same time. When the time for orgasms comes near, it is by far better for both partners to concentrate on satisfying one partner at a time; usually the female having an orgasm first is more desirable. Females can sustain sexual activity after orgasm while men have difficulty doing so. Females need plenty of time as well. They will know their orgasm is the prime concern of both partners and the male partner will know that once his partner's orgasm has taken place, his pleasure will be prolonged and he can have a successful ejaculation with the help of his partner.

A TECHNIQUE FOR FEMALES WITH COPD

Position is extremely important. Prop yourself up against the head of the bed with pillows or, if necessary, sit in a chair. Your lover must bring the part of his body to be stimulated to you. You must indicate to him what he is to do. For instance: gently guide his mouth toward yours. You are capable of licking with the tongue while breathing through your mouth. Take one section of the body at a time so there isn't constant movement required by your partner. Your lover can sit or kneel next to you, facing you. Give quick kisses, flicks of the tongue, and delicate touches over each area of the body you want to stimulate. Use your imagination. Guide his body to the right position. As you are stroking, kissing, and licking other parts of the body, begin to manually touch the head of the penis and gently stroke your hand over the testicles. If they are up high and tight, your lover is highly stimulated and an ejaculation may soon occur. If you wish to prevent this, decrease the amount of stimulation that you are giving. Hold your hand still or hold the testicles lightly. You can also gently put your fingers around the top of the testicles and pull them down. This will decrease excitement. If the penis is not fully erect or if you wish to increase stimulation, put the thumbs and forefingers of both hands around the penis and stroke away from the middle, squeezing lightly as you do that. Don't squeeze too hard, or you will decrease erection. As you are stimulating your lover, ask him where would he like to be touched? How hard? How fast? Remember, at this point you are giving him pleasure. Both of you should concentrate on that. Oral sex is not out as a possibility for you. Have your lover stand beside the bed and bring his penis to your mouth as you sit comfortably. Breathe through your mouth and stroke with your tongue and use manual stimulation at the same time. Remember, the head of the penis is the most sensitive, the shaft the next sensitive, and lastly the scrotum. Keep checking the testicular elevation and gauge the degree of excitement by that and the firmness of the erection. Continue to stroke and caress and lick the penis until the erection is hard and firm. There is no rush! It may take a long time, but don't get anxious. When you both mutually agree, either by word or gesture, that it is time for ejaculation to take place, you may have to stroke in a very firm manner for which you may not have the strength. Let your lover put his hand over yours and let your hand go limp. Let him set the pace and force of your strokes. Ejaculation will soon occur.

Another good position for you is with your lover lying on his back with his head toward the foot of the bed and his penis within hand's reach. While you sit propped up comfortably. If you wish to complete intercourse by having the penis in the vagina, try the woman-on-top position or gently slip off the bed, putting your knees on the floor and supporting your chest on the bed. Your lover can then enter from the rear. You can also turn on your back, put your knees up, and use the traditional position of the man being on top. He should take special care, however, to support his weight on his elbows and knees.

So take your time; don't be afraid to use oral sex; avoid the maneuvers which require you to hold your breath for a long time; be happy and adventuresome about your task! Both partners, at this point, should concentrate on giving the male his orgasm.

Although we described bringing the male to orgasm first, we actually advise the woman receiving her attention first. Assume your most comfortable position, as described in the previous section. Your lover can be kneeling or reclining beside you or sitting next to you. Try to assume a position in which both your clitoris and vagina are reachable for manual stimulation. Sitting up with knees flexed gently is fine. If you can lower yourself onto pillows in a semivertical position or sit on pillows on a chair, this should provide adequate entry to your genitals. Let your lover know by the way your body moves how stimulated you are. You should not be afraid to correct him immediately if his stroke is too fast or is painful. Let him know gently what is right for you. Both of you should concentrate on giving you pleasure. You might want to put your hand over his and gently guide him to stroke your clitoris until your level of arousal reaches its climax. Also, your lover can insert his finger into your vagina and locate your G spot to give you additional pleasure. (The G spot is a small round firm area inside the vaginal opening on the anterior wall.) You may prefer simultaneous stimulation of the clitoris and the G spot, or alternating stimulation of these areas. If you wish to have your partner put his penis into your vagina, assume one of the positions described above.

There is no reason why the male cannot be brought close to ejaculation and the female then be brought close to orgasm and positions changed to allow the penis to be inserted into the vagina if that is what you both wish. However, it may be difficult and not always best to achieve simultaneous orgasm. We recommend that the male partner bring you through orgasm if possible and then insert the penis into the vagina; you could at the minimum have additional pleasurable sensations from this. Although you may want to use penis in vagina, remember, it's not necessary. Each of you can have a satisfying and pleasurable experience without actual intercourse in the traditional sense.

A Technique for Males with COPD

Position is extremely important for the male with COPD and is the key to success. Prop yourself up against the back of the bed or sit in an armless chair. Just as with the female, it is important for you to guide your partner's body toward you. Read the section on the female. The same principles apply. You can give short kisses and use your tongue and still breathe with an open mouth. Don't rush your partner. There's plenty of time. Use her stimulated appearance and the joy you are giving her to stimulate yourself while you are giving her pleasure. When it comes time for more intense stimulation, a good position for the woman to assume is on her back with her head toward the foot of the bed, her knees flexed, her genital organs facing you. If she wants, her clitoris can be stroked easily and effectively, and your finger can be inserted into her vagina to stimulate her G spot. Watch the movement of her body. If she moves toward you, she is finding the sensations pleasurable and her arousal is increasing. If she moves away, back off. The clitoris is extremely delicate. Let her put her hands over yours and show you her magic spots and indicate to you the pace and the force with which she wants to be stroked.

To practice oral intercourse, you could kneel on the floor facing your partner. She can lie on her back on the bed with her genitals just in front of your mouth. You will have plenty of air to breathe in this position. Remember to watch her body. If she is lifting her pelvis toward you and is lying comfortably and relaxed, she is enjoying herself. If she pulls away, you are making her uncomfortable. Ask what you can do. Is this too fast? Am I too firm? Remember, at this point you are both concentrating on her pleasure. Anything she indicates to you is the right way. To bring a woman to orgasm through clitoral stimulation, usually no extra firmness or particular strength is required. This can be done with the tongue or with the fingers. If, however, you are having trouble achieving the ultimate goal, your partner should put her hand over yours. Your hand should go limp and she should direct the pace and firmness of the stroke until orgasm is achieved.

To have an orgasm with COPD, stay in a position that feels comfortable. Your partner has free access to your body whether you are sitting in a chair or propped up in bed. Be relaxed, unafraid, and enjoy yourself. Indicate any movements which are not pleasurable. Correct these movements immediately. Don't be afraid to communicate! Do it freely, gently, and firmly. Read the principles in the previous section. They apply to you as well. If you are having trouble achieving ejaculation, you can guide your partner's hand or her mouth. She may be kneeling in front of you, or she may be on the floor in front of you, as you sit in a chair or on the edge of the bed. Any way you are comfortable is acceptable. If you wish to enter her vagina with your penis, here are some recommended positions: Your partner can lower her vagina onto your penis while you sit. If you like, you can stand while your partner leans over a bed or table and you can thus make a rear approach. This position does require more energy expenditure. Remember once again, you don't need to have intercourse in the traditional sense to have wonderful sexual experiences. You can have the ultimate orgasm by manual or oral stimulation. You just have to be willing and open-minded enough to do it.

Covering every possibility is beyond the scope of one chapter. However, you can use the principles you've learned here and experiment for yourself. If you want, find books which graphically demonstrate sexual positions. Accept what you like; reject the rest. Find ways to stimulate each other at the same time and/or concentrate on ways for the both of you to concentrate on one partner at the same time. Don't forget communication! Leave any bitter or angry remarks out of the bedroom scene. If you have any real criticisms, save them for a time well after sex is over. The postcoital period is a time for further talk and romance, not for corrections or criticisms. Consider developing your sexuality a lifelong task. Work hard at it and the rewards will be great.

8

Conservation of Energy, Relaxation Exercises, and Panic Training

Here are five top-priority activities we want you to concentrate your energies on:

1. Eating right
2. Working out regularly
3. Getting as much sexual stimulation and satisfaction as you need
4. Participating as a member of your own health care team
5. Keeping your mind alert and stimulated

These areas require your urgent daily attention and commitment. In all other activities you want to conserve energy and do things as quickly and as efficiently as possible. You want to have enough zing left over for the top-priority items. You want to eat a great diet, but you want to expend as little time and energy as possible cooking and shopping. You want to dress well and have clean, nice-looking clothes, but you don't want to spend hours hand-washing fussy materials. You want your house clean and dust-free, but with no time to cook and certainly no time to scrub clothes, you definitely don't want to spend a great deal of time and energy doing housework. That's what this chapter is all about: conserving time and energy. Look at our five top-priority items, and we hope you'll notice that these are the activities essential to a great life for anyone. Look at someone you admire, let's say an executive in a top company. If that person doesn't have the time to prioritize these activities, we don't think he's "living well." Now that you've got the general idea, let's get down to specifics.

CONSERVATION OF ENERGY (COE) FOR PERSONAL HYGIENE

You want to be sure to take good care of your teeth. Infected and broken teeth lead to poor nutrition because of inability to chew properly and comfortably, and multiplication of germs which in turn can infect your lungs.

This is as good a place as any to tell you how to make our special invention—a bib-style holder. Take a chain designed to keep you from losing your eyeglasses and attach metal electrical clips to each end. Sling the chain around your neck and attach to it any appropriate length of paper toweling. You can use your special bib when practicing COE in the bathroom, and it will be equally handy for keeping your clothes clean while eating. We'll mention it again in the section on COE for housekeeping.

Obtain a rechargeable electric toothbrush (soft bristles) and a rechargeable electric shaver. Set up a personal hygiene center consisting of a comfortable chair, a table with mirror, World's Fair brand round toothpicks, dental floss, disposable cups, a shaver, and necessary combs, brushes and makeup. At your sink have paper cups, a toothbrush, and paste. When it's time, obtain the toothbrush and paste from the sink, along with water. Sit comfortably at your personal hygiene center and shave first. Here's the right way to brush your teeth: Angle the brush up for the upper teeth so that the ends of the brush gently massage the gum line and the base of your teeth. Angle the brush down for the bottom teeth. If your inner jaw is narrow in the center, you can hold the brush vertically. The major problem with teeth at your age is the presence of plaque, a gritty substance you can feel with your tongue at the base of your teeth near the gum. Plaque control is essential if you want to retain the teeth that you have and prevent gum disease. Most teeth from middle age on are lost from gum disease and not from cavities. As you hold the brush over each section of your teeth, count slowly to ten. Finish by brushing the chewing surfaces. You are sitting comfortably —take your time. You need a full three minutes. When you have finished brushing, it's time to use dental floss to clean the loose triangles of gum tissue between teeth. Wind eighteen inches of the floss mostly around the middle finger of one hand and the rest around the middle finger of the other, leaving a few inches in between. Use your thumbs and forefingers to guide the floss gently between the teeth. When the floss reaches the tip of the triangular gum flap, curve the floss in a C shape against the tooth. Move the floss five or six times up and down along the side of the tooth gently, going under the gum line until you feel resistance. Without removing the floss, curve around the base of the adjoining tooth and floss that one, too. Turning your middle fingers brings you fresh floss. Take another three minutes. Take care not to injure your gums when either brushing or flossing—gums are delicate. Lastly, slide your tongue over the brushed areas. Put finishing touches on the job by using a toothpick. Gently slide the toothpick at the base of the tooth and remove any gritty substance you left behind. (Don't hurt your gums.) Once you've finished at your hygiene center, return to the sink, empty any cups you've used, and rinse your mouth. You might like to have a dental irrigator also. Using the lowest setting, you can aim the jet tip between your teeth to remove any final particles, using a constant side-to-side motion. It's also convenient to use around bridgework. You should practice oral hygiene at least twice a day and preferably after each meal. You can floss and use toothpicks in bed in the evening if that's more appealing.

You can conserve energy by having a chair or stool to sit on in the shower. Exchange your old shower head for a hand-held shower which can be switched to a variety of delightful sprays. It will not only be easier to clean yourself without getting your hair wet or water in your ears, you will also be able to use the shower head to rinse off the walls of the shower and the bathtub. And besides, a vibrating massage is a luxury you'll appreciate after a brisk exercise session. We recommend that after you shower you use standard-size towels rather than heavy bath towels that may be luxurious but fill with water and are difficult to launder.

Don't rush your bowel movements. Once eating is over, a gastrocolic reflex occurs. This means that the large bowel gets stimulated by food in the stomach. Therefore, after meals might be an easier time for defecation. The occasional use of simple glycerin suppositories available at any supermarket or drugstore may help you avoid straining and decrease the work of breathing during the act.

Do as many of your personal hygiene tasks as you can while wearing your pajamas. If you get a little toothpaste on your pajamas, it's not nearly as difficult to live with as getting the same stain on other clothes.

A special note: Now might be a good time to take a renewed interest in your appearance. We highly recommend a snappy new haircut, one that's attractive without requiring much maintenance or frequent visits to the hairdresser. Women may want to try using some makeup that will look great and not take much time or energy from the morning's routine. (Hypoallergenic cosmetics are readily available if needed.) A few simple changes can make both men and women look better and *feel* better—and you're worth it.

COE IN THE KITCHEN (OR HOW TO COOK WITHOUT COLLAPSING FROM THE EFFORT)

The kitchen is not a good place to get your exercise. In fact, contrary to popular opinion, the kitchen is a good place to take it easy. You don't want to use up a good deal of your precious energy making meals and then be too tired to eat them. If you have too many dishes, ingredients, or cooking utensils, if you get overheated or overtired, you simply won't cook. You will be tempted to eat junk foods and delicious garbage. You also won't have enough energy left over for the important things described in this book. Unless cooking is the love of your life, read this chapter carefully and learn how to cook with a minimum of effort. Tasty food, however, is one of the true joys of life, so the aim of this section will be to show you how to make the tasty and nutritious meals described in Chapter 4, "Body Business." Stick to the Healthy Core diet. Don't vary breakfast and lunch at all for weeks or months at a time. The foods and recipes we have given you in Chapter 4 provide a great diet with little or no preparation. Don't worry about getting bored with the food. You're free of the drudgery of complicated cooking and extensive cleanup.

Set your mind to using a minimum of mixing and measuring tools. Our recipes will require little or no mincing, chopping, or other complicated maneuvers.

If you need oxygen, bring it into the kitchen. If necessary, obtain fifty feet of tubing. You may need that anyway to walk around your house comfortably during the day. It would not appear wise, however, to have oxygen in your nose when using an open flame. We recommend that you do not use a gas stove while using oxygen—it's just too risky. Luckily, however, you really don't need any stove, and you certainly should not be bothered with an oven. Ovens change the humidity in the room; they require bending and lifting of heavy, hot pans. The well-equipped kitchen for the pulmonary patient has a toaster oven with a pop-out shelf, an electric frying pan (Teflon-lined), an electric can opener, a blender, and a second electric frying pan with a rack in it for steaming or a Teflon-lined electric wok to use as a steamer. If you can, buy a microwave oven and an electric warming tray.

Put your electric frying pan next to the sink in such a manner that you can lift the handle, leaving the front part of the frying pan on the counter, and dump residue right into the sink. Never put away your electric frying pan, blender, toaster oven, electric can opener, or any other piece of equipment that you find valuable.

Get out your favorite spices and leave them out where they can be easily reached. A good beginning combination is onion powder, garlic powder, oregano, bay leaf, thyme, pepper, paprika, and curry. If you want to use salt, put one level teaspoon at a time in a small, clear glass shaker. You will want to know how much, i.e., how little, you are using. Leave flour out in a small canister or shaker container.

Have several rolls of paper towels placed at strategic spots in the kitchen. Have small wastepaper baskets lined with disposable plastic bags also placed in important spots around the kitchen. You must be able to dispose of paper towels, napkins, bones, and other garbage directly at your feet. We're aiming for a minimum number of steps.

A liquid multipurpose glass, appliance, and cabinet cleaner should also be in evidence.

Obtain a heat-sealer, boilable and freezable cooking bags, and a felt-tip marking pen. Cook an extra portion each night and seal it in a bag. If you do this for one week, the following week you'll only have to boil water and drop in a bag to make your main dish.

Get breakfast, lunch, and dinner ready all at the same time. We recommend preparing three meals just before dinner. Dirtying the kitchen and cleaning it up once in twenty-four hours is all that's necessary. You will be cooking dinner for that day and breakfast and lunch for the next day. Do not vary breakfast or lunch from the Healthy Core diet menu for weeks or months at a time. Free yourself from worrying about what you're going to eat for those two meals.

Begin by getting your main meal cooking. *Now* try the *three-tray system*—one tray for each meal. Here are some suggestions for breakfast and lunch.

Tray 1 contents (breakfast):

1 paper cup filled with skim milk
1 paper cup filled with All-Bran or other equivalent high-fiber cereal
1 paper cupcake holder filled with low-fat cottage cheese (your "butter")
Roll or slice of whole wheat bread
1/2 grapefruit
Napkin, grapefruit spoon, teaspoon, cereal spoon, knife

Tray 2 contents (lunch):

Pita sandwich with low-cholesterol Lite-Line cheese, 1 tbsp. peanut
  butter (if allowed), and lettuce
Carrot
Cucumber
Sweet pepper
Tomato
Apple
Knife, spoon, napkin

Cover all appropriately and place the trays in the refrigerator. If
one tray is smaller, you can fit the breakfast tray on top of the lunch
tray and carry it all in one easy trip (and it will take less space in the
refrigerator).

On your counter have two disposable cups with a tea bag or in-
stant-drink powder. The above menu is for the 1500-calorie Healthy
Core diet. Consult Chapter 4, "Body Business," for other appropriate variations.

In the morning take tray 1 from the refrigerator. Stop off at an
electric coffee pot that was turned on by an inexpensive timer and is
now filled with hot water. Add the water to the appropriate cup and
take tray 1 to the table. You will have one trip to the table going and
only one trip coming back. Throw the disposable plates and cups out
in a convenient basket on your way back to the kitchen. Use the
same system with trays 2 and 3 for lunch and dinner.

During week 1 make dinner five nights for double the number of
people who eat it. If you're one, for instance, cook for two. Seal one
portion in the boilable cooking pouch and freeze. Week 2—just boil
the bag and steam your vegetables. Label the bags with the felt-tip
marker. (Be careful not to buy bags that are bigger than you need.)

On the day you shop, do not cook. That's a good time to eat out or
consume a high-quality prepackaged dinner. Try to limit yourself to
buying foods with ten grams of fat or less per serving as listed under
the nutritional analysis on the label. Eat out or use prepared foods
one other night per week, but keep the sodium content of this meal in
mind.

When you cook dinner at night, limit the number of utensils you use to one to three. Use no more than one electric frying pan, and another as a steamer. A wok can be used for stir-frying *and* steaming. Remove any excess grease or oil from your pans by using a wad of paper toweling. Virtually eliminate all chopping, mincing, and cutting.

Learn to look at recipes critically and change items which increase work; adapt recipes to your own use. For instance, for sliced onions, use frozen chopped onions or onion powder; for minced garlic, use garlic powder; for fresh peeled, seeded tomatoes, use canned stewed tomatoes; for potatoes, use canned boiled potatoes.

You can also utilize a powdered egg substitute. These are cholesterol-free and can be used in place of eggs in many recipes. You can substitute Fleischmann's Egg Beaters or similar for eggs. They are cholesterol-free, have no shells, last a whole week in the refrigerator, and keep in the freezer. They are full of good, high-quality protein.

Make special arrangements right now for those days on which you don't feel well. You should have on hand at least a one-week supply of powdered, high-calorie foods, such as Meritene (try drugstores), whose packages state that they contain 100 percent of the recommended daily allowance of protein, vitamins, and minerals. Even though some of these are sweet, you may not be able to eat when you don't feel well, and in this way you'd be able to keep your nutrition up.

You should puree meat, soup, and vegetables in a blender and pack them in boilable-freezable bags or other freezing containers, label them, and put them in the freezer. If you can only eat liquids, at least they will have a familiar taste and be as nutritious as regular foods. Have powdered milk and canned milk on hand and vacuum sealed bags of dried fruits and nuts.

When cooking, use no measuring spoons or cups.

Substitute the following for measuring equipment. You already know how much a cup is: the amount of water you pour in when you make yourself a cup of tea or coffee. If you're not sure, take the pans you are cooking in, such as your electric frying pan or blender, and pour one cup of water in there now and see what the level is. That will be a cup every time. Think about things as a shake, a long pour, which is about three seconds, or a short pour, which is to tip the bottle and flip it back again. A couple of heaping tablespoons is a small handful. If you're not sure, measure it once.

Protect your clothing in the kitchen and in fact while eating. You don't want a lot of wash. Use the bib we described in the personal hygiene section. Roll out a longer length of paper (or clip on a towel or cloth napkin). You have an instant, disposable apron. Use caution with a paper bib near the stove. (By the way, you should take the same little gadget with you to restaurants and use the restaurant napkin. Ask for an extra napkin for your lap. Recently we went all over New York in very good restaurants and used this little gadget. People didn't even care and some asked us where they could buy one.)

Don't use anything but paper towels in the kitchen. Buy the least expensive brand.

In all of your cooking, think: How can I make the minimum amount of dishes and mess to clean up? How can I take the minimum amount of steps? How can I minimize lifting, twisting, bending, chopping, and cutting? How can I make an entire dinner using only one or two pots and perhaps a spoon and fork?

To find idea models we recommend eating in good, moderately priced restaurants. They must make beautiful, tantalizing dishes, but they cannot afford long-drawn-out recipes. Look at the way the food is presented. Taste the sauces. Bring a notebook and draw yourself a sketch of the way food is served and ask them to share some of the details of their recipes with you.

You've got to team up COE in the kitchen with the chapter on the Healthy Core diet. It's easy to do. You can have a lot of fun and provide great nutrition, too.

COE FOR HOUSECLEANING

COE for housecleaning means having a lightweight electric broom, a rechargeable electric hand-held vacuum, a lamb's-wool duster with an 18- to 24-inch handle, a lightweight Hoky or similar carpet sweeper, a general all-purpose liquid appliance and cabinet cleaner in a plastic spray bottle, a hospital magnetic-type dust mop (as large as practical), and a nice long paper towel bib. You may need a bucket to hold all your equipment.

In the bathroom, have paper towels and appropriate cleaner right out in the open. If a cleaner is too strong (don't whiff it up close), dilute it with water.

The time to clean the bathroom is immediately after use. Wipe off the sink and faucets with the cleaner immediately after using the bathroom. Likewise, wipe down the shower quickly with a squeegee mop that you've left there. Use your toilet brush once a day. Use liquid soap in the bathroom, bathtub, and shower to prevent soap buildup in the soap dish.

Your real enemy is dust. Armed with your lamb's-wool duster, electric broom, lightweight carpet sweeper, and hand-held vacuum, you can prevail. Wear a mask, such as 3M Brand Nuisance Dust Mask, Cat. No. 8651, Auto Part No. 3202. Make war on dust daily.

Make sure there are mats outside your front door for removing dust and other debris from shoes.

A rubber foam squeeze mop should be adequate for doing kitchen floors.

For spills and stains, saturate the stain with liquid cleaner and wait. Let the chemical do your work for you.

Your bed is a critical place. You want it comfortable, but you don't want to spend a lot of energy fixing it up. We call this our hypoallergenic conservation of energy bed. Put plastic zippered covers over the box spring and mattress and over each of those put a fitted sheet. Leave the fitted sheet on the box spring indefinitely. Ideally, an electric mattress pad (also known as an electric sheet) goes on next on your mattress, over that a fitted sheet, a top sheet, a hypoallergenic lightweight blanket, and then a lightweight short comforter (no feathers). The latter will act as both a bedspread and a blanket. You will be perfectly warm and comfortable in all weather without having heavy blankets resting on your body.

When arising in the morning, grasp the top sheet, blanket, and comforter, which weigh only a few ounces, and with one tug pull them up under the pillow, pat, and your bed is made. An alternate way to make your bed is to leave the comforter and sheet at the bottom of the bed folded over. When you get into bed you only have to pull the bedclothes up.

To change the sheets, put a chair or bench near the foot of the bed. Lay the comforter and blanket back on it. Change the fitted bottom sheet on a different time schedule from the top sheet so you'll only have one sheet and a pillowcase to wash at one time. The first and third weeks of the month you might want to change the bottom sheet and the second and fourth weeks of the month the top sheet. Use the occasion of changing the bedclothing to make extra sure that dust is not accumulating under the bed.

COE FOR SHOPPING

Map out the supermarket according to your Healthy Core shopping list. Go blithely past the huge varieties of foods. You don't require any variation to know you are eating well. For staple items, which include toilet paper, bathroom tissues, napkins, paper towels, foam plates, and cups, we suggest bulk buying. Go to the Yellow Pages and find a dealer who will deliver a half or whole case of these items. If you have a storage problem, you'll have to work around this idea. We bet there's a closet somewhere in your house stuffed with clothes you never use. Get a family member or friend to go with you a few times a year to buy other staple items such as soap, toothpaste, soap powder, and cleaning solution. Make a list of any items that you know do not spoil and that you can buy in bulk in advance. This will make your weekly shopping load much lighter.

Buy frozen foods, particularly vegetables, in large bags in which vegetable pieces are each frozen singly. You can take out as many pieces as you want at a time. Boxes of frozen vegetables are handy if you are cooking for more than one person, but may be less convenient to use for a single portion.

Try to find a grocer who will cut meat the way you want it cut, with a minimum of bone in a small enough portion, and who possibly can deliver. It will be worth the extra money. If not, make friends with the butcher in your supermarket. He can be very accommodating.

Do most of your clothes shopping by using catalogs such as those from Sears or J. C. Penney. For everyday, think about wearing a jumpsuit made of a blend of cotton and polyester. This will be lightweight, washable, and look very spiffy; it can go almost anywhere; and with a one-piece item you're dressed and ready to go. You could have one jumpsuit that you don't wash very often and use for housecleaning and other chores. Don't buy any clothes that are not colorfast (including socks), and don't buy any clothes, unless you like to torture yourself, that can't go in both the washer and the dryer. All washing instructions should be the same on your clothes, something like "Wash Under Warm and Tumble Dry Medium." Make sure all your clothes are permanent-press, with no ironing whatsoever required. The same goes for your sheets. If you have an iron, bury it.

Use the Yellow Pages. Phone ahead. Don't go to a store unless you know you have a good chance of finding the item you want. Get as many items as you can delivered. Bank by mail whenever possible. Use a bank next to your supermarket or grocery store. Consider keeping a month's worth of "cash" in traveler's checks.

COE FOR WASHING CLOTHES

COE for washing clothes means buying the right kind of clothes that we've just told you about. Now here's how to make it even simpler. Obtain two to six mesh laundry bags. As you use your underwear, put T-shirts or bras in one, shorts or panties in another, and socks in a third (or if you're not that fussy, put all the dirty underwear in one bag). When the bag or bags are moderately full, drop the entire bag filled with soiled laundry into the washing machine. When washing is completed, take the bag out and put it in the dryer. When drying is completed, do not empty your clothes out of the bag. Hang the bag or bags on pegs and take out your clothing as you need it. Don't worry if your underwear is wrinkled: a small price to pay to free yourself from so much drudgery. Just think—a minimum of effort at the washer-dryer. Wash everything at the same temperature, e.g., warm wash and warm or cold rinse. Dry everything under medium. If you happen to be washing only towels, then you might want to go to a hot drying cycle. Wash towels and sheets together, shirts, slacks, and underwear together. Use one kind of color-safe detergent.

COE FOR DAILY ACTIVITIES

General COE for daily chores means not bending at the waist. Bring any items to your midsection, putting your center of gravity there for lifting, using both arms if possible. Bend from the knees gently. Pull an item along the floor or counter rather than lift it. Do any chores you can sitting down. Make work centers for yourself and have all equipment for a task in a central place and leave it there.

COE for keeping current may mean not buying a daily newspaper (possibly a bother to get and a lot of waste to get rid of), but rather using the TV or radio to keep up with daily news. You can subscribe to a weekly magazine such as *Time* or *Newsweek*.

Reading is extremely important and mentally stimulating. To keep up with reading novels we suggest subscribing to Books on Tape or a similar service. Call 1-800-626-3333 to obtain a catalog. "Read" novels while doing postural drainage or during relaxation periods.

Let timers work for you: for instance, a timer on the TV set so you can fall asleep without getting up, a timer to turn your lights on in the morning and off in the evening. There are inexpensive timers available for your thermostat, and other timers can be attached to room heaters to make sure that a room is warm and comfortable before you enter it and then cools down after you customarily leave it, e.g., your dining room. You can save on fuel bills and yet keep a comfortable, stable temperature as you move from room to room in the winter. Air conditioners may also be regulated by timers.

Your daily chores may require you to climb stairs. If so, figure out how few trips a day you can make. Plan your day and your week. Make a list of necessary tasks, using the principles shown to you above applied to other activities of daily living that we may not have covered.

Incidentally, here's an easy way to walk up the stairs: Breathe in standing still, walk up about three stairs while breathing out, using pursed-lip breathing if comfortable. Stop a moment, breathe in, and then continue. Your stop may be long or so momentary that no one notices it, but if you need COE walking up the stairs, try this method.

COE FOR MEDICATIONS

COE for medications means opening your bottles just once a week yet never missing a pill! Obtain one to four different colored, divided, one-week-size medication dispensers (one for each time of the day you take medications). Label the dispensers for the appropriate times with a felt-tip pen. Not only are you now all set for a week, but you'll also be able to know if you forgot to take any of your pills. (Fig. 32)

HOW TO BECOME A PACKAGE DEAL

Have you ever noticed that successful people are surrounded by other people insuring their good looks, their nutrition, and, in general, their pleasing presentation to the world? Think about the President of the United States surrounded by advisers, speech writers, publicity agents, and campaign workers. Think about your physician with his office aide and faithful secretary. Successful people are package deals. You too can become a package deal. Will your neighbor do

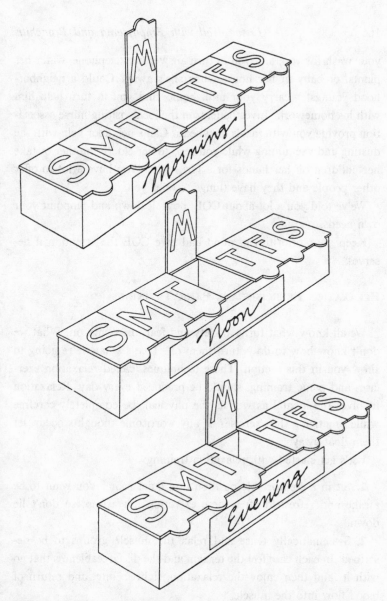

(Fig. 32) COE for Medication. Put a week's supply of medication into the dispensers labeled by day and time. You need a separate dispenser for each time of day you take your medications.

your wash for you, and you in turn answer her telephone, water her plants, or baby-sit her house when she's away? Could a neighborhood youngster carry your milk home, and you in turn help him with his homework? Investigate. Can the local visiting nurse association provide you with meals on wheels? Can a neighbor help with the dusting and vacuuming while you read to her elderly mother or take her children off her hands for a few hours? You have a lot to offer other people and they have things to offer you.

We've told you a lot about COE; now sit down and pinpoint your own needs.

Keep your priorities in mind and give COE the attention it deserves.

RELAXATION EXERCISES AND PANIC TRAINING

We all know what turns anxiety and fearful feelings on. What we don't know how to do is turn them off. That's what we're going to show you in this section. These techniques, called relaxation exercises and panic training, should be practiced every day. Relaxation involves the mental as well as the physical. Be completely carefree while practicing the exercises. If any worrisome thoughts occur, let them float away.

Let's get started with relaxation training:

1. Sit in a comfortable position in a quiet room. You want to be awake and refreshed after these exercises, not asleep, so don't lie down.

2. Systematically tense and relax the muscle groups to be described. In each case feel the tension and the disagreeableness that go with it, and then enjoy the relaxation, light feeling, and return of blood flow into the muscle.

3. At the end of all the relaxation exercises, if any part of your body is still tense, do those exercises again.

4. In each case, while contracting or tensing the muscle, slowly

count "one one-thousand, two one-thousand, three one-thousand" to yourself and then relax for a similar or slightly longer count.

Here are the specific maneuvers:

Make a fist with the right hand. Count—relax. (Remember, study the tightness, the tension; squeeze the muscles to the count of "one one-thousand, two one-thousand, three one-thousand," and then note the feeling of lightness, relaxation, and blood flowing back into the muscles.)

Make a fist with the left hand. Count—relax.

Bend the arm at the elbow, feeling the tension in the upper arm. Right arm first, then left arm. Count—relax.

Grasp the left shoulder with the right hand and pull, feeling the tension in the right lower arm. Count—relax.

Grasp the right shoulder with the left hand, feeling the tension in the left lower arm. Count—relax.

With the feet flat on the floor, push the toes away, feeling tension across the top of the feet. Count—relax.

Curl your toes upward, producing tension in the front of the shin. Count—relax.

Squeeze the buttocks together and feel tension across the back of them. Count—relax.

Push the abdomen out as you breathe in, as though you were filling it with air. Count—relax.

Arch the back forward and put your shoulders back, producing tension in the lower back. Count—relax.

Contract your abdominal muscles. Count—relax.

Bite down with your teeth, clenching the jaw, and then allow the mouth to fall slightly open. Count—relax.

Put your tongue to the roof of the mouth, feeling tightness in the tongue and on the top of the mouth. Count—relax.

Wrinkle the forehead and the nose, feeling tightness across the face. Count—relax.

Grimace, pulling the lips back and feeling tightness across the mouth. Count—relax.

Now feel as though you are floating on a cloud, and think of your own secret word that means "calm" to you. Repeat it in your mind. Feel as though you are being supported by the cloud. Count backward from five to one slowly.

Are you relaxed? Did you answer no? If so, have you had the right mental attitude toward these exercises? Remember, in many cases it can be easier to be tense and fractious than calm and happy. Your job is to work on the latter.

Don't expect to break bad habits overnight. Practicing COE and relaxation techniques in all of the multivaried activities of daily living may sound simple when you read it. Don't get discouraged when you try to incorporate them into your daily routine and find out that it takes a lot of discipline. Keep working at it. Each time you find a system or idea that works, grasp it, change it, make it your own, and integrate it into your personality and your routine as soon as you can. Take one idea or a half a dozen ideas, whatever you can work with comfortably; then go on to improve yourself with practice.

Before you know it, with each task you have to do, your mind will begin applying COE techniques.

Keep practicing relaxation exercises. Give them the few moments a day they deserve.

Panic training is for those times when relaxation exercises aren't sufficient: those times when you find yourself breathing fast with rising fear you can't control. Rapid, shallow, uncontrolled breathing is very ineffectual, as you well know by now; it will merely drop the pressure in the bronchial tree and cause airway collapse. Begin panic training today. If possible, sit down at a table, and rest your shoulders and your head quietly on the table top. Support your feet by having them rest gently on the floor. Push the chair slightly back from the table so you are sitting up and leaning slightly forward with your shoulders on the table. This will expand the rib cage. Use the secret word you invented for relaxation training that means "relax" or "be calm." Tell yourself, "——— down." That means relax, let go, stop grabbing at the air. Allow more time to breathe in. You might want to hold your breath at the end of inspiration as you count "one one-thousand, two one-thousand," and then allow more time to breathe out. Try to let your belly wall balloon out as you breathe in to allow more room for the diaphragm to drop. Purse your lips gently on expiration. Practice slow, even breathing; this will keep up the air pressure in the bronchial tree. It will allow more time for the oxygen to cross over that delicate alveolar membrane into the bloodstream before you breathe out. Transfer the same feeling of relaxation of body from relaxation exercises to relaxation of breathing. If you exercise and know your training sensitive zone, otherwise known as a safe pulse range, you will have less of a reason to panic. You will know what is a safe pulse range for you, and you will learn that one of the most important things to learn from an exercise program is how to pace yourself. Long before panic, if you think that you're beginning to grab at the air, check your pulse. The pulse is a very sensitive indicator of the status of the cardiopulmonary system. If your pulse is over your safe range, slow down before panic sets in. If you are not near a table, then try sitting and using the same respiratory maneuvers.

Practice relaxation exercises once a day and panic training once a day and use both techniques in tight situations—relaxation when you're tense, and panic training when short of breath. With practice you'll become quite an expert. You'll be able to save the situation and avoid unnecessary distress.

You should control your emotions; they shouldn't control you. Remember, with conservation of energy, relaxation, and panic training, you are using as little energy as possible on necessary but unimportant tasks in order to have all the energy and *joie de vivre* necessary for the important things in life.

9

Hospital Stays—Ignorance Isn't Bliss

A hospital's a place where you can depend on someone for every conceivable need at any conceivable time. There's a difference, however, between total, blind dependency on others and trusting capable professionals you know can help you. Lack of knowledge fosters fear, and fear may lead to unnecessary suspicions, poor cooperation, and often panic. You can become a hazard to yourself. *Believe us, ignorance isn't bliss.* When hospitalized, no matter how sick you are, you *must* continue to be a member of your own health care team. To that end we want to tell you about the professionals and procedures you may encounter when hospitalized.

NURSES

Nurses are in charge of seeing that the ward runs properly and that the orders of the physician are implemented. Nurses also administer direct care to patients. An important function of the nurse that you may not know about is to make clinical decisions as to changes in your condition. She is your guardian while you are on her ward. She will spend much more time with you during the day than the physician. It is the nurse's responsibility to note changes and to call the physician, and that responsibility is important and not a little awesome. It behooves you, then, to communicate freely with your nurse. Don't "save" things for your doctor. It is a common practice for the doctor to come to the ward and check with the nurse first and review your chart. If she knows your symptoms, she will tell them to the doctor and he can think about your problem as he walks to your room.

RESPIRATORY THERAPISTS

Respiratory therapists are highly trained members of your health care team, specializing in the use of equipment and techniques necessary for the treatment of respiratory disease. This includes equipment used to administer bronchodilators deep into the bronchial tree and the performance of chest physical therapy. They may assist you not only with treatments for bronchodilation but also with postural drainage, chest percussion, vibration, and cupping, if ordered by your physician. You may be familiar with these techniques from your own home pulmonary toilette regimen. (If you don't have to practice postural drainage at home and you are asked to do it now, you should be familiar with the use of gravity to facilitate drainage. At times, your head and shoulders may be put in a position lower than the rest of your body. This may be necessary because the exacerbation of your COPD has resulted in excessive mucus production.) Respiratory therapists understand pulmonary disease; they are also in a position to note changes in your condition and report them. Communicate freely with your respiratory therapist. Along with the nurse and the physician, he is a partner in your health care.

CONSULTANTS

A consultant is a physician whom your doctor feels knows more about some aspects of your problem than he does. A good doctor knows when to ask for help; no doctor can know everything. If your doctor asks for a consultant, think more of him and not less. A consultant may see you and just write his suggestions on a separate sheet, or he may become an active member of the treatment team in your case. Either way is acceptable. Just make sure that a take-charge person is running the show and that somebody is coordinating the suggestions of your consultant or consultants, since in some cases several consultants may be involved.

How to Impress Your Consultant

Impressing your consultant is easy: Give him a history (your story) that he can understand, so he can get right to the heart of your problem. For instance, when the consultant asks you "What brought you to the hospital?" don't answer, "A taxi." The doctor is starting the search for the reason that you've had to be admitted. This is called the *chief complaint* and is the beginning of your history. Ninety-five percent of all diagnoses are made by history as opposed to physical examination. Here are all the parts of a proper history. You should know them and practice being able to express yourself. There are minor variations among physicians, naturally, but essentially this is the manner in which a physician investigates your problem.

The chief complaint is a brief statement describing the events which resulted in your hospitalization. For instance:

DOCTOR: What brought you to the hospital?
YOU: For four days my cough has been getting worse and worse in spite of taking antibiotics and adding steam and postural drainage.

At this point the doctor may want a brief description of other relevant facts about you, including your age, marital status, occupation or previous occupation, the names of any other diseases you have, and the length of time you have had pulmonary disease. When he "writes up" your case, the first sentence may read as follows: "This is a fifty-five-year-old, married, retired truck driver with mild diabetes who has had pulmonary disease for eight years and enters the hospital now with chief complaint of four days of increasing shortness of breath and uncontrolled cough in spite of intensification of pulmonary toilette and the addition of antibiotics to his regimen."

This opening sentence, ending with the chief complaint, sets the stage for the description of the rest of your history.

History of the Present Illness. In this section you tell your story in detail. Look how much the doctor already knows about you, including a knowledge of your home situation, whether you have a help-mate in life or not, your occupational exposure, how long you've been sick, and what symptoms were uncontrollable. Your doctor may now say, "Well, how did this all start?" You should begin your story by describing this relapse rather than your entire pulmonary history. On the other hand, you want to give the doctor an indication of how you feel when things are going well, so you might begin by telling your story something like this:

YOU: I felt the way I usually do. I bring up about two tablespoons of sputum each morning and I'm quite active. Then I noticed that my sputum began to increase in volume. I phoned my doctor, and he told me to take my on-hand antibiotics and to increase my updraft nebulizer treatments to every four hours from four times a day. Nevertheless, my sputum volume continued to go up, and my sputum became thick and turned a greenish-yellow, and I felt as though I couldn't get it up out of my chest. My breathing became difficult and I had a constricting feeling in my chest.

DOCTOR: Then what happened?

YOU: Nothing helped. So my doctor suggested that I be admitted to the hospital.

DOCTOR: What has happened here in the hospital?

YOU: My sputum volume still seems to be high and the color is off. I'm constantly wheezing and have a constricting feeling in my chest, and I feel exhausted and anxious, as though I'm not getting enough air. This morning I had such a violent coughing spell that I became terrified.

In this part of the history you give the consultant the facts concerning what has happened from the onset of this relapse until the time he has seen you. Respond to the doctor's questions directly and succinctly. He may have many other ancillary questions regarding your current medications, home regimen, functional capacity, etc.

Once you are done telling the doctor all the relevant details of this portion of your present illness, he may want to know the rest of your pulmonary history. This is also considered part of the present illness, but is usually discussed at this point, after the acute phase of your problem is covered.

DOCTOR: When did you first begin to notice you had a pulmonary problem?

YOU: About five years ago, after smoking for fifteen years, I noticed that I became short-winded with exertion.

At this point the consultant may want a summary of how much difficulty you have had with your pulmonary disease. He may ask about previous hospitalizations, their relative dates, and the reasons for admission. If you cannot memorize these, you should have them written down.

Other Relevant Medical History (Past Medical History). In this section of the history you would be asked to discuss all other diseases that you have, such as diabetes, high blood pressure, and heart disease. Your consultant will ask you directly. Have the information at your fingertips. He does not need to know the exact year or date, but he does need to know the relative year, the medications that you take and their exact dosages. It goes without saying that if you've read this book you know the names of all of your medications and treatments, and the doses that you use. You should explain to the doctor how you manipulate medications if you've been allowed to do so with permission and what the usual effects change of medications has on you. For instance, if increasing your prednisone (steroid hormone) alleviates your wheezing and shortness of breath within a few hours, your consultant would like to know it, and if increasing your theophylline preparation by one tablet a day produces nausea, he'd like to know that, too.

Other important parts of the history which your consultant may or may not ask you include your family history, about your mother, father, siblings, and children. He may want to know what diseases they have and whether they are living or dead, and, if deceased, at what age they died. He might also ask about your work history (occupational history); social history, including use of alcohol and cigarettes; allergies to medicines and other substances; or any unusual exposures to inhaled chemicals, fumes, or particles.

The last section of a history is called the review of systems, and if it's relevant for you, the doctor may ask you questions about every other "system" in your body, such as, Do you have any trouble with your head, eyes, ears, nose, or throat? Do you have any nausea, vomiting, diarrhea, or constipation?

You might want to practice writing out your history. Here's an outline to use as a guide.

Opening sentence: Age, sex, race, occupation, marital status.

Chief complaint: What's happening.

History of the present illness: Recent events; details of the entire course of your pulmonary problem; medications: names, dosages, times taken, their effects; other hospitalizations.

Past medical history: Other major illnesses, any surgery or medication. Previous hospitalizations: why, where, what dates. Immunizations.

Family history: Mother, father, siblings, children. (Living, dead, their diseases and allergies.) Include significant diseases in other family members.

Occupational history: Include former and present jobs, especially those involving chemicals, fumes, dust, etc.

Social history: Hobbies; smoking; alcohol; activities; exercise, and usual functional capacity; education.

Allergies and adverse reactions: Include known allergies and also "bad seasons" of the year when wheezing or cough is intensified. Describe any adverse reactions to medications, places, animals, food, chemicals, etc.

Review of systems: Other medical problems or symptoms not already mentioned.

You can ask your own physician to review your history to ensure that it's clear and accurate. Always keep a copy with you. It might also be important for you to have copies of final summaries of previous hospitalizations.

Try not to ramble. Now that you know all the parts of the history, you don't have to be afraid when the doctor at first only wants to know about what's happened to you in the last few days or hours that he won't ask about some other facts that you feel are very relevant. You'll get your chance to talk to the consultant and give him all the facts. He needs his chance to get the facts down in a comprehensible order so he can design your treatment plan quickly and properly.

You can certainly impress your consultant favorably, but now—what impression will he make on you?

How to Evaluate Your Consultant and Get Your Money's Worth

You might think we're going to say that a good consultant is one who spends a great deal of time in the room talking to you. Not necessarily so. A good consultant is probably a popular one, and he may have a fast, quick mind and be able to synthesize facts rapidly. On the other hand, a slow and steady mind may be equally effective. So you can't judge a consultant by how many minutes he spends with you. Your doctor has put your pertinent history on the chart and the consultant may indicate to you that he knows many of the facts, but he should spend time talking to you and checking out the pertinent facts, looking for those clues that may have been overlooked or have suffered from underemphasis. A good consultant finds out for himself. When you're speaking to him, he should be giving you his attention, especially when your responses are clearly organized and relevant to your present problem. A good consultant at least does those parts of the physical examination that are pertinent to your problem, such as listening to your chest, asking you to cough, checking your legs and neck veins. You should notice him looking at you and checking your overall demeanor. When you ask him a sensible question, he shouldn't hesitate to give you an answer you can understand. If you've read this book, you understand your disease and you're in a position to comprehend what he's telling you. If you don't, ask him to explain himself again. A good consultant has a clear picture in his mind of the problems involved in COPD. He should be able to give you an answer you can understand. A good consultant might also tell you that he doesn't yet know what's wrong with you. Always admire the physician who admits he doesn't know. That's OK. It's when he doesn't do something about it that you know you're in trouble.

How to get your money's worth? You've already done it. You've given the consultant a thorough history, the tool he needs to do the best job he can.

BRONCHOSCOPY

Reading this will soothe your nerves. Almost all bronchoscopies are now done with a fiberoptic instrument rather than a rigid steel one. The fiberoptic bronchoscope contains thousands of glass fibers which carry light and images. The instrument has a flexible tip that is controlled by the physician and can bend to a considerable angle both forward and backward. It provides a direct look inside the bronchial tree without requiring surgery. There is a special channel in the bronchoscope for suctioning secretions and instilling medications, including local anesthetics. Tiny brushes and biopsy forceps can be passed through the channel to obtain specimens from suspicious areas. The fiberoptic scope can find out why you coughed up blood or why your pneumonia won't "clear up." If thick secretions are stubbornly plugging your bronchial tree, small amounts of mucus-thinning agents can be instilled followed by suctioning, resulting in an unobstructed airway.

Most of the time you'll be wide awake during the procedure. Only a mild sedative is necessary. The discomforts are minor—the possible gains major. Don't be afraid. (Fig. 33)

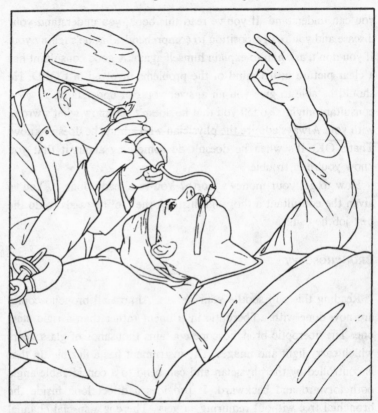

(Fig. 33) Flexible Fiberoptic Bronchoscopy. Discomforts are minor. Most of the time you will be awake.

INTUBATION, VENTILATION, AND TRACHEOTOMY

Sometimes the going gets rough and your doctor might feel that he is "losing control over the airway." That means he feels that you may not be getting enough oxygen in and carbon dioxide out to sustain life adequately. The situation usually occurs when there is a large volume of secretions plugging the bronchial tree and no amount of postural drainage, suctioning, antibiotics or other measures have helped. Usually you have become exhausted because the work of breathing against this large resistance is so great. If that happens, you might be in for one or all of the big three: intubation, ventilation, and tracheotomy.

The bad news is that it is frightening, uncomfortable, and you can't talk when intubated. The good news is that you will be safe, feel more relaxed, can communicate by writing, and can put yourself in other people's hands with confidence.

For intubation a semirigid, soft plastic tube is inserted either through the nose or mouth down through your voice box (larynx) into the upper part of the trachea. For one method of intubation the doctor will stand behind you, lifting the base of your tongue out of the way so that he may see the larynx to insert the tube. He needs to use a metal instrument for this called a laryngoscope. Another technique requires the tube to be inserted down through the nose. Once the tube is inserted into the trachea, a soft balloon is inflated to fix the tube in place and permit air to be ventilated into and out of the lung without a leak around the tube and also so the contents of your stomach cannot get into your lungs and choke you. When this happens, no air can vibrate your vocal cords, so you cannot talk. At first, the tube may feel horribly uncomfortable and may make you cough. Substances which will suppress the cough can now be put down the tube and you will soon adjust to it. Intubation provides a clear channel to suction secretions out and, once having accomplished this, to get that miracle substance, oxygen, in.

Once intubated, a ventilator is usually necessary. This machine assumes the work of breathing and is attached by simple connectors to the endotracheal tube. Once on the ventilator, you should feel relaxed, as though the strain was off. Let them know if you are not getting enough air in or out. Remember, this situation is uncomfortable, but you are now safe. Try not to panic and fight the machine. The ventilator is a machine which is tried and true and extremely reliable, and you have an excellent chance of survival with no loss of function. A clipboard with a pencil and paper will allow you to communicate with the staff. (Fig. 34)

If you require mechanical ventilation for a more prolonged time, a tracheotomy may be necessary. Fortunately, this is an uncommon

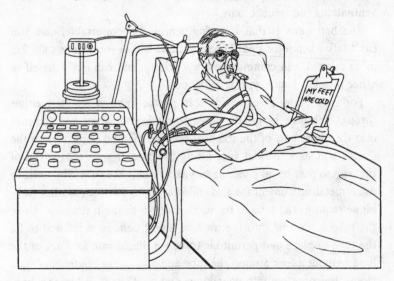

(**Fig. 34**) Mechanical Ventilation. You can communicate in writing while on a ventilator. Be calm, stay in contact. Know the day and time. Ask for your glasses and a clipboard and pen.

requirement. In this procedure a small hole is actually made through the neck in the trachea and an airway (or tracheotomy tube) is inserted into that hole. This airway functions in the same way an endotracheal tube does to allow for suction of secretions and connection to a ventilator if necessary. It allows you to eat. (Fig. 35) A tracheotomy may also be done when intubation is impossible for any reason or when there is an obstruction which has to be bypassed.

If you have to be intubated or have a tracheotomy and be put on a ventilator, your job is to be calm, let people around you know that you are in contact, and inform them when you do not feel the flow of air is proper. You must also keep yourself oriented. If it is in view,

(Fig. 35) Tracheostomy. A tracheostomy allows you to eat.

look at the clock. Know what day it is. Wear your glasses. It's also important to try to move your legs in bed at least every hour. If possible, ask your doctor to have bedside PT, i.e., physical therapy. Ask to sit in a chair. You may be able to ask to walk a few steps with a therapist using what is called a manual ventilator. This soft, squeezable bag can be attached to the endotracheal tube or tracheotomy tube to assist your breathing while walking. (Fig. 36)

Once your secretions are cleared out and infection and exhaustion are over, you will soon be "weaned" from the ventilator. This is usually done gradually by removing the ventilator and attaching the endotracheal tube to a tube delivering oxygen. Sometimes the dials on the ventilator are set so that in effect you are breathing on your own. There are many procedures for weaning, but rest assured that as soon as possible the medical team taking care of you will gradually remove the support mechanisms. Once the endotracheal tube is re-

(Fig. 36) Walking with Manual Ventilator Assist.

moved, your voice might be a little hoarse, but you'll be able to speak immediately. The same is true for the tracheotomy tube. The hole it leaves will close over naturally, leaving an inconsequential scar.

We hope that understanding these procedures and knowing that they are safe and effective, with few side effects, will help to keep your spirits up if you should have to go through this difficult and trying time. Remember, you can make it. Don't let despair defeat you.

GETTING OUT OF BED TO GET WELL

You may have a vision of yourself in the hospital lying in bed being cared for by a pretty nurse in a starchy white uniform. Forget it. The hospital is no place to sit around in bed. If you really want to get sick, if you really want to get pneumonia if you don't already have it, or if you want your pneumonia to get worse instead of better, you'll lie in bed thinking that's the way to get well. You must be as active as your doctor will allow in the hospital. If you usually walk with oxygen, insist on a small portable tank so that you can take your walks. If you need help to walk and nobody comes to take you on a regular basis, ask your doctor to write it as an order so that you'll be walked on a schedule, let's say four times a day, just as you'd be given a medication. Ask for a physical therapist to come and help you if necessary. Just one day in bed produces significant weakening of muscles. You don't want to lose all that you've gained in terms of fitness and training. Get someone to bring your weights, get your jogging shoes out, and, as much as you can, be active.

Landing in the hospital is not the most pleasant of experiences. However, you are there to get well, and your chances of survival are much greater in the hospital when your doctor feels that you belong there. Cooperate, keep your spirits up, and as we said, keep active. Understanding who's who and what's what should help you to feel more comfortable with the hospital environment. If you land there, good luck—benefit from it—but try to get out as soon as you can!

WHAT TO TAKE TO THE HOSPITAL IN AN EMERGENCY (A QUIZ)

Now here's a final exam. Problem: You feel terrible, but you have enough energy to gather a few things to take to the hospital. Essential items are (more than one answer is correct):

1. Toothbrush
2. Comb

3. Bathrobe
4. Walking shoes and socks
5. Books
6. Glasses
7. Copy of your history
8. Candy
9. Razor blades

The correct answers are 4, 6, and 7. The hospital has plenty of items for personal hygiene such as toothbrushes, combs, and razor blades and books and magazines are readily available. You need your glasses to keep oriented and be able to see well. A copy of your history will help your health care team, as we've described. The indispensable items are your walking shoes and socks (yes, the very same ones you use in your exercise program). They'll help you to be active again as soon as you can and show the staff you have that fighting spirit.

10

Leisure, Work, and Travel

THE PIE OF LIFE—LOOK HOW WE'VE SLICED IT UP

Look *hard* at our pie. (Fig. 37) Does your life have all the same pieces? Are you missing pieces? Or perhaps you have a slice we haven't thought of. Do you agree with our pie? We hope not, because there is something definitely wrong with it. . . . The slices are all the same size. The recipe for "live well" pie should contain all the necessary ingredients, but the amounts have to vary. That is, the slices must change according to the natural requirements of activities and their import to you. At this point, we'd like to ask you to mentally make your own pie of life, including all the activities you do daily or almost every day, varying the slices according to your present real-life situation. In the next and final chapter we'll develop this idea further. In the end, you'll make your own variation, right for you. Now let's turn to leisure activities.

BEING ACTIVE

How to be as active as you can? Force yourself. Doing nothing is easy. It's also boring, depressing, and degrading to the human spirit. Doing something is harder. It's also invigorating, uplifting, inspiring,

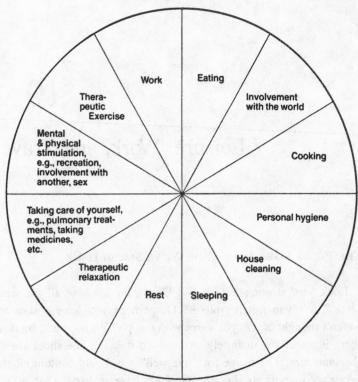

(**Fig. 37**) Life Is a Pie: Look How We've Sliced It Up. There are twelve essential ingredients in the recipe for "live well" pie.

and ennobling to the human spirit. Keep going. Use rest periods, relaxation exercises, panic training, and your training sensitive zone as aids, but keep moving. Risk a little. After you've pushed yourself to do something, ask yourself if it was worth it. And if it was, push yourself some more. If it wasn't, change the activity.

Force yourself to do the things you find worthwhile. When you think you've "had it," try this: Get in your most comfortable position for ten minutes. Can you change your mind, and go ahead? You might be wondering, what has pushing myself got to do with a chapter on leisure anyway? We're not talking about driving yourself when you're short of breath, but rather about those times when you feel like sitting around and vegetating. Recreation is a necessary part of *every* day, and having fun does take effort. We want you to understand and think about the kinds of recreation that are available to you and at the same time give consideration to the "size of the slice" that makes sense for you.

ENERGY COSTS

One MET (metabolic equivalent) is the energy expenditure at rest, or, more simply explained, the amount of oxygen required while sitting quietly. Normally, it is 3.5 milliliters of oxygen per kilogram of body weight. That is to say, the heavier you are, the more oxygen you need both at rest and with exercise. You may burn more than 3.5 milliliters of oxygen per kilogram of body weight at rest because your work of breathing may be increased. Nevertheless, for our purposes we will say that one MET will be considered baseline energy expenditure at rest for you. There are many worthwhile activities that require virtually no energy expenditure above one MET. We define these as activities for hand and mind. Energy expenditure increases as activity increases. Running burns approximately ten METs, and this is the average maximum number of METs which a vigorous person can expend. Activities with energy expenditures higher than one MET will be grouped as recreation for hands, mind, and body and will be given numbers from two to ten, representing the relative need for oxygen above the resting level, e.g., ten METs is ten times the resting oxygen requirement. You can't take these values as absolutes. An expert tennis player may require fewer METs to play than a novice. It's helpful, however, to think about activities in terms of their energy cost to you as being at or above your resting level.

Recreation for hands and mind includes knitting, crocheting, needlepoint, embroidery (acceptable activities for men as well as women in this day and age), reading,* assembling electronic kits, rug hook-

* Reading, strictly speaking, doesn't involve the hands, but it is a great one-MET activity.

ing, macramé, and similar activities. Think how nice it is to give someone a present you've made. It says, "I'm back in this world." And what about making something for yourself? Other one-to-two-MET activities include playing cards, chess, and checkers.

Since we separate therapeutic exercise from recreation, vigorous activities are not required. Engage in as many recreational endeavors as please you and at levels of physical activity that are comfortable and appropriate. Recreation means fun—do whatever gives you the feeling of having it. Remember—it's *right* to have fun every day.

Now what about a home computer? For a small expenditure, you can open up a whole new world: learn to program, keep track of your diet, daily physical examination, budget, and finances. For a little more you can hook by phone to computers around the country and communicate with other computer operators.

Have you ever thought of drawing, perhaps just with charcoal, or watercolors or acrylics? What about oil painting? (See precautions in Chapter 3 under Self-protection.)

Keep yourself in projects. Have something to take up with your hands *every day*.

Activities for hands, mind, and body include swimming if you know how (if you use oxygen, get your long tubing and leave the tank on the side of the pool). Can you take up golf again, for two to three METs with a power cart, or three to four pulling the bag. Light shoveling and gardening takes five to six METs. Don't forget going to movies, shows, concerts, national historic sites, and museums. As a point of reference, splitting wood is about six to seven METs. Jogging, seven to eight METs. Moderate basketball, seven to eight METs.

We consider sex a recreation (an orgasm is four METs).

Eating out is an important and pleasurable activity. Set the MET count yourself, depending upon how dressed up you get and how difficult it is to get to the restaurant. If you need oxygen, put it over your shoulder or pull it behind you without feeling self-conscious. If people look at you, they're being curious, not mean, the way they'd look at any interesting person. If you catch their eye, give them a big smile. If you feel like it, take the little bib chain we described earlier and ask for an extra napkin. Put one on your lap and attach one to the chain. Just be sure you sit in a no-smoking section. Try not to overeat. Restaurants usually serve about twice as much food as you ordinarily require for a meal. Why not eat half and ask for the rest in a "doggie bag." It'll be one less meal to cook, and you won't come out bloated and wake up with bags under your eyes the next day.

Here's how to stay on your Healthy Core diet and still enjoy yourself:

First course: Light soup such as vegetable or French onion without the cheese or croutons.

Second course: Salad—dressing on the side. Pick dressing closest to Italian and spoon on 2–3 teaspoons.

Main course: Broiled fish, minimal butter; baked fish, minimal crumbs and butter (ask for margarine if available); baked potato, sour cream on the side, use 1 teaspoon sour cream; vegetables—skip if oily.

Dessert: Fresh fruit, frozen yogurt, or skip this course and have a nice fruit at home with a hot drink for you and your friends.

If the main course must be meat, don't eat the fat.

WORK TO YOUR HEART'S CONTENT

What is a section on work doing in a chapter on leisure? Work seems to have more in common with fun than with any other activity in this book. It requires an active mind, possibly an active body, involves you as a citizen of the world, is elevating to the human spirit, and adds to self-esteem and efficiency. If you already have a job, try hard to keep it. You may have to sacrifice some time for recreation or limit recreation to hands-and-mind forms for a short time each evening. If you work in a service-type profession, such as in a hospital or in a professional office, that may be sufficient involvement with others and may supplant that activity altogether. If you no longer have a job, what about trying to start a new career? How about a telephone answering service, child care, mail order sales, secretarial or typing services? Could you learn to bake one item, such as a pie, and contract for its sale to several restaurants? You don't necessarily need to do much of the physical activity of baking and delivering yourself once you make the contacts and sell the idea. Or try the federal government. Your "handicap" may actually get you a job. Is there a service you could perform for a neighbor, even if it is only for an hour a day? Remember, people who do any kind of a job well are always treated with dignity. You can't work? Don't be bothered by that. Remember, the benefits (mental and physical stimulation and satisfaction) of leisure activities are identical to those of work. With either work or leisure you ought to learn how to network. Here's what networking is and how it works.

NETWORKING

Let's say that you decide that photography would provide satisfying leisure or occupational activity. It's not just enough to take pictures. You could also join a photo club. Once you've met other members and made friends, this is a good time to plan a hike or a walk or a field trip to take more pictures. Now make a set of slides to show at club meetings. Finally, can you volunteer to teach photography? Learn to network with all your recreational activities if it's possible; particularly involve that one significant other as much as you can.

So now you know that networking is a technique in which you utilize activities to meet other people, expand your horizons, begin new activities, and so greatly enrich your life.

TRAVEL

Travel should be considered when you have long periods of stability and you have an excellent understanding of your disease and self-care. Your physician can provide you with the names of other physicians from various reference books such as the American College of Chest Physicians Membership Directory. If you use oxygen, you should ask your local supplier to call ahead and make arrangements for you to have an adequate supply at your destination. Take more than enough medication and copies of your history with you. Avoid places that are so remote that there is no way to get any help if you need it. Railroad and bus lines allow you to utilize your own oxygen. A driving trip in your own car or van offers you maximum flexibility.

Here's some additional information you may need if flying. The air pressure in a plane at thirty thousand feet is similar to that on earth at six thousand feet above sea level. You may therefore need oxygen to fly, though you don't need it on the ground. Your physician can decide. Should you need oxygen, you must notify the airline at least forty-eight hours in advance. No personal oxygen can be carried on any U.S. airline; some foreign carriers do allow it. Any portable tanks must be emptied and stored as luggage. Should you have a stop over and need oxygen on the ground, you must make additional arrangements. Once again, check with your supplier.

Only nebulizers with leakproof (gel-cell) batteries can be used aboard planes.

Request the no-smoking section and an aisle seat near the rest rooms. Move your legs around frequently during long flights. The humidity in the airplane cabin is only 10 to 12 percent, so drink enough fluids. Unless you have other special requirements, order diabetic meals; they are calorie-controlled, low in fat and sugar, and usually have fresh fruit for dessert.

The International Air Transport Association (2000 Peel Street, Montreal, Quebec, Canada, H3A2R4; Phone 514-844-6311) will supply you with the standard medical information form to be completed by your doctor. Keep one copy with you.

Lastly, think carefully about your needs at your destination. You might need a wheelchair in addition to oxygen.

Utilize the same principles of energy conservation and expenditure that we've been discussing throughout this entire book.

If you are extremely stable, you might consider the grand adventure of a July cruise to Alaska. Recently, we traveled aboard the SS *Universe* and noted the following: The ship goes along the inland passage, and without leaving a protected, glassed-in deck one gets a constant panorama. When it's not raining, the humidity is low and the temperature a delightful high 60's to low 70's. The pollen count at sea is zero. It's not really necessary to do more than walk around the towns and not really necessary to leave the ship to thoroughly enjoy the trip. There was a physician, a nurse, and oxygen on board, but if you require constant oxygen, you must make your own arrangements, making sure that oxygen would be available if you should need a refill or that you take a sufficient supply aboard. There is a national distributor network for liquid oxygen. You should look to your supplier anytime you want to travel. He should be able to supply you with additional portable containers and central tanks as necessary for this or any other trip. We made such a call to our supplier. We found that if an empty central tank could be flown to Vancouver, the usual departure point, there was a dealer able to provide a full tank. You should know exactly how long your tank will last at the liter flows you use. It's possible that for a trip such as the Alaskan one you might need two central tanks. You must discuss your situation directly with the passenger liaison officer. When we interviewed that officer on the *Universe,* she was very open to having people with COPD aboard, as were the physician and nurse.

Difficulties may arise because a hospital is not immediately available. On the other hand, you are not too far from land at any one time. The incline of the gangplank, depending upon the water level, may be steep, but it is also short. You will really have to watch your diet and let them know in advance about such things as skim milk. You can bring your own low-cholesterol cheese slices aboard along with other special foods and keep them in a small foam chest filled with ice, which is automatically supplied to the rooms several times a day (you supply the chest).

On this particular cruise there were three professors aboard discussing the oceanography, geology, and history of the area. There was also a full library and a librarian. The cruise itself was "laid-back." You would not require more than one or two dress-up outfits. Otherwise, a Windbreaker, a plastic poncho, a sweater, and the usual shirts and slacks would be adequate. Don't forget your jogging shoes and a copy of your medical history, including a list of your medications.

You also need to be either near an elevator or able to climb stairs. Once again, a frank talk with the passenger liaison officer will put you in a cabin which you as an educated pulmonary patient know will fill your most pressing needs.

There are many extra paid side trips offered. In general, we don't recommend long trips on buses. There is no place to stretch, the carbon monoxide level may rise, and the sites visited may be remote. Be content to take city tours and walk through the streets. You need easy access to the ship. Another option is to rent a car with another couple.

If you love scenery, nature, whales, eagles, mountains, fjords, glaciers, clean air, and you understand that there could be bad weather, possibly somewhat rough seas and some remoteness from a hospital, the adventure of a cruise up the Alaskan inland passage can provide the thrill of a lifetime.

Don't consider it without your doctor's permission.

A WORD ABOUT PETS

Pets are a joy and a commitment. You have to be careful with dander, feathers, and other allergens that are a part of being an owner of some birds and animals. A poodle grows wool, does not shed or have dander, and might be called nonallergenic. You have to be able to make sure the dog can exercise outside the house. Perhaps you have a yard, a chain, or a run, or a neighborhood youngster who can do that for you if you cannot fulfill that commitment. Tropical fish or goldfish make wonderful pets, but don't provide the affection that a dog can. Cats are ideal in some ways because they need not go out. However, cat dander is too frequently an allergen for cats to be recommended. Consider a turtle, iguana, or snake. Does that sound far out? The cold-blooded snake can be a warm and friendly pet.

What's happening here? We've made leisure seem like work, and work seem like leisure.

Life's funny, isn't it?

11

Summing It Up

Have you given some thought to how you would slice up your pie of life? Good. In this chapter we've translated those slices into functional reality and provided you with something that every important person has: a daily agenda. Successful people budget their time, set priorities, conserve energy, have fun, exercise, and eat right. Just like you! Is the agenda below the only one for you? Of course not. But it's a model to set your own variation by.

AGENDA FOR LIVING WELL

7:00–7:30 A.M.	Out of bed, morning treatment while listening to the news
7:30–8:00 A.M.	Breakfast
8:00–8:15 A.M.	Physical exam and record results
8:15–8:45 A.M.	Housework
8:45–9:15 A.M.	Relaxation exercises
9:15–10:00 A.M.	Dress, shave, shower—don't forget plaque control
10:00–11:00 A.M.	Exercise walk, followed by weight lifting
11:00–11:30 A.M.	Change clothes and recover
11:30–12:15 P.M.	Recreation

12:15–12:45 P.M.	Noon treatment while listening to a book on tape
12:45–1:30 P.M.	Noon meal and cleanup, plaque control (optional)
1:30–3:45 P.M.	Involvement with the world
3:45–4:15 P.M.	Rest followed by panic training
4:15–4:45 P.M.	Late-day treatment while listening to a book on tape
4:45–5:45 P.M.	Prepare breakfast, lunch, supper
5:45–7:00 P.M.	Dinner and once-a-day kitchen cleanup, plaque control (optional)
7:00–9:00 P.M.	Evening activities—include cleaning respiratory therapy equipment, using inspiratory muscle trainer
9:00–9:30 P.M.	Evening treatment while listening to a book on tape
9:30 P.M.	Personal hygiene—don't forget plaque control—and ready for bed

This is an agenda for a nonworking day. If you work, then you obviously must make adjustments in this schedule. You may have to forgo involvement with the world and consider that work fulfills this obligation. You will have to do your exercise walk either in the morning before work or right after. If you work, certain other duties might be delegated to others, such as cooking and housecleaning. Your requirements for exercise, recreation, eating right, taking care of yourself, however, do not change. A word about involvement with a single other person. We did not discuss this separately because that involvement should be woven as much as possible into the fabric of your entire day. Try to involve the closest other person in many of your activities, and you should involve yourself in theirs.

Have you noticed that we've had to "double up" on some activities, like doing pulmonary toilette and listening to a book on tape? Can't help it! You're a busy and successful person!

A FINAL MESSAGE

> Ah, but a man's reach should exceed his grasp.
> ROBERT BROWNING

Dear Reader:

We know we've made it all clear and easy. Right? Wrong!

We hope we've made it clear, but we can't make it easy! Changing habits is oh, so difficult. Don't let despair take hold. Everything in this book may not work for you—sift, accept, discard, invent.

Think—talk—do.

"Living well" is being open-minded, optimistic, energetic, romantic, disciplined, committed, forward-looking, and heroic.

"Living well" *isn't* being cynical, sad, tearful, reminiscent, and pessimistic.

Be a pro—do your best, even when you don't feel like it.

Never lose hope, never stop growing.

We wish you good luck—and great success.

With much love,
BERTON and MYRA SHAYEVITZ

For the Physician

This book reflects the optimism we feel in our own rehabilitation efforts with patients with COPD. We find the sicker the patient, the more likely he is to devote himself to the program. In fact, the sickest patients make the greatest relative improvement. Therefore, we exclude virtually no one from any part of the rehabilitative effort.

In Chapter 1 we introduce such sophisticated concepts as inspissated secretions, ventilation perfusion inequality, airway collapse, and enzyme destruction of tissue as graphically as possible. By the conclusion of the chapter the patient should know enough medical terminology and pathophysiology to communicate effectively.

The book is intended to supplement and not to substitute for the patient's physician, and every effort is made in this book to increase effective communication between the patient and his doctor.

Current scientific information on smoking as the major cause of chronic bronchitis and emphysema is presented, as well as the effect of airways dysfunction in nonsmokers chronically exposed to tobacco smoke, such as the patient's children or grandchildren. Recent studies have shown that effective counseling by physicians, augmented by printed material, increases the proportion of successful quitters. We advise abrupt cessation, i.e., quitting cold turkey, as probably the most effective method for smoking cessation. There is a contract to be signed in the presence of five significant others to deepen commitment.

In the chapter entitled "The Treatment," we introduce the patient to three diaries. The first is recorded after a daily self-examination. We teach the patient how to take his pulse and respiratory rate; grade his sputum by volume, color and thickness; check for edema; take his temperature by touch; grade wheezing and overall functional capacity, and record the results in what is called the self-evaluation diary. The patients become quite astute in detecting significant differences in their physical examination.

The therapeutic manipulation chart is actually a detailed patient instruction form in which the patient records the medications he takes and with your permission varies them under preset circumstances, e.g., taking on-hand antibiotics for an increase in volume of secretions or an extra tablet of diuretic for a weight gain of over three pounds.

The patient is asked to show you these diaries for you to make additions or deletions.

Finally, the patient is given a relapse progress diary in which he records "what went wrong" and what measures were taken and what the final outcome was. This should provide valuable follow-up information when future relapses occur.

There are sections on commonly used medications and the proper use of the metered dose inhaler.

A daily pulmonary toilette regimen is described.

In "Body Business," basic information about nutrition and food groups is detailed. The diet prescribed presents what we call a "healthy core" of foods which provide one gram or more of calcium, up to two grams of sodium, and less than 300 milligrams a day of cholesterol in a diet high in fiber, high in complex carbohydrates, and high in vitamins A and C (to follow the recommendation of the National Research Council), and with adequate protein to cover moderate stress states in most cases. Diets of 1200, 1500, 2000, 2500, and 3000 calories are given. Simplified shopping and cooking lessons to demonstrate adequate nutrition with minimal effort are offered.

The patient is also given some simplified tests of body composition to help determine calorie requirements. The diet chapter also offers practical advice on what foods patients can prepare simply without skimping on good nutrition.

Studies have shown that some pulmonary patients tend to have low muscle mass and suffer from malnutrition of the marasmic type. In these poorly nourished patients, body weight and diaphragm muscle mass have been reduced to 70 and 60 percent of normal, respectively. Poor nutritional status has been associated with severe respiratory muscle weakness distributed both in inspiratory and expiratory muscles. We therefore stress adequate caloric as well as adequate protein intake while limiting sodium, fats, and junk foods, but we realize much more research is needed in this field.

In the chapter on diet the specific need to increase activity while increasing protein to provide increase in muscle mass is stressed.

Exercise has, more than any other aspect of our rehabilitation program, shown tremendous implications for the patient with COPD. We find exercise to be the single most effective tool that we have. We find that the pulmonary patient needs an exercise heart range (in this book referred to as the training sensitive zone) just as any cardiac or any other middle-aged adult who undertakes a conditioning program. We regularly do treadmill testing on most of our patients, measuring oxygen saturation by ear oximetry at the same time. If the patient is unable to walk more than a few yards without stopping, we stress-test using three liters of oxygen to start with unless there is a contraindication. We then provide the patient with a training sensitive zone as close to 70 to 85 percent of predicted MAX with three to four liters of supplemental oxygen. Administration of supplemental oxygen has been shown to improve exercise tolerance significantly in patients with chronic obstructive pulmonary disease, and our experience reinforces this finding.

The patient transfers the training sensitive zone from exercise to activities of daily living in addition and uses it as an effective tool to fight panic and anxiety and increase the quality of his life-style. Recently, half the respondents to a questionnaire stated that before participating in our exercise program, their activities of daily living were predicated on fear of overdoing. All of that half stated that this was no longer true since being involved in a formal exercise program.

We find that providing the patient with an exercise heart range, or training sensitive zone, at 70 to 85 percent of predicted MAX, with supplemental oxygen if necessary, provides him with not only the increased physical advantages of increased endurance, but also the psychological "high" experienced by other individuals who exercise. Adherence to these programs, once commitment is made by the patient, is excellent. Our patients, whether they exercise in our center or at home, fill out the exercise diary as provided in the chapter on exercise and mail the diaries on a regular basis for perusal by the physician. A simple twelve-minute walk test is described to the patient to provide an estimate of progress.

Here are our suggestions for writing the exercise prescription. If the stress test indicates ischemia, then after proper cardiac workup we use 85 percent of achieved or ten beats per minute below level of angina or ischemia as the upper range.

If ischemia is not present, we try to set the lower range as close to 70 percent of predicted MAX as possible and the upper limit as close to 85 percent of predicted MAX as possible with three to four liters of supplemental oxygen if desaturation occurs. If desaturation with supplemental oxygen occurs at or below 85 percent of predicted MAX, then we pick the next highest possible heart rate, allowing a safe margin of about ten beats per minute. We instruct patients to keep to the lower limit of their training sensitive zone as much as possible. If the functional capacity is very poor and/or a stress test is not appropriate, you may eliminate the lower limit from the exercise prescription and designate only a safe upper pulse rate.

Initially, the amount of time spent in the training sensitive zone should be one to two minutes or one half the treadmill time.

There is included an upper-body weight-training program using light weights, and instructions for the use of the inspiratory muscle trainer. Recent research indicates patients showed increased respiratory muscle endurance following inspiratory resistive training.

Social isolation, anxiety, depression, and what D. L. Dudley has called the emotional straitjacket—unwillingness to express any emotion because of inability to handle the resultant physical symptomatology—characterize some of the psychological problems of the patient with COPD. We make an attempt in the chapter "Psyche" to show the patient how to overcome these obstacles in a multifaceted program consisting of exercise, utilizing the training sensitive zone as a "safe range" to fight panic; a knowledge of their disease to keep control; and involvement with others to relieve isolation. The patient is introduced to the concept of enlightened self-interest and increasing involvement with the outside world and given practical suggestions which he can conceivably follow.

The chapter on sex graphically depicts sex as a normal and desirable body function. We have tried to give the patient a detailed description of sexual technique utilizing methods which we have found effective over the past twenty-five years. The ventilatory limitations of one partner are always taken into account, and we find that increased sexual activity, even that which still remains short of actual intercourse, enhances both the physical and mental well-being of the patient.

Chapter 8 describes conservation of energy techniques in shopping, daily life, personal hygiene, during housework and clothes washing, and in the kitchen. Relaxation training and panic training are also described.

Should the patient be hospitalized, we have described the role of nurses, respiratory therapists, and consultants, and procedures such as suctioning, bronchoscopy, tracheostomy, intubation, and ventilation. We have encouraged the patient to take his walking shoes to the hospital with him and to remain as active as you will allow him to be while there.

In "Leisure, Work, and Travel," the patient is introduced to the concept of METs and low- and moderately high-level activities and encouraged to enjoy recreational activities on a daily basis as being therapeutic.

In the final chapter we help the patient to set an agenda and to plan his day around necessary activities such as exercise, appropriate diet, pulmonary toilette, and recreational and vocational activities. We point out that his day can be a busy and successful one.

We hope this book serves a needed function in helping to provide a high quality of life for the patient suffering from chronic obstructive pulmonary disease. We urge patients and physicians to help begin programs of pulmonary rehabilitation, for we have seen heartening results.

Selected References

GENERAL

BURROWS, BENJAMIN. "An Overview of Obstructive Lung Diseases." *Medical Clinics of North America* 65 (May 1981): 455–71.

CHODOSH, S. "Examination of Sputum Cells." *New England Journal of Medicine* 282 (April 1970): 854–57.

DOLOVICH, M., R. RUFFIN, D. CORR, and M. T. NEWHOUSE. "Clinical Evaluation of a Simple Demand Inhalation MDI Aerosol Delivery Device." *Chest* 84 (July 1983): 36–41.

DULFANO, M. J., and C. K. LUK. "Sputum and Ciliary Inhibition in Asthma." *Thorax* 37 (1982): 646–51.

FINDLEY, LARRY J., DONNA M. WHELAN, and KENNETH M. MOSER. "Long-Term Oxygen Therapy in COPD." *Chest* 83 (April 1983): 671–74.

HABENICHT, HERALD A., LAWRENCE PREUSS, and ROBERT G. LOVELL. "Sensitivity to Ingested Metabisulfites: Cause of Bronchiospasm and Urticaria." *Immunology and Allergy Practice* (August 1983): 25–27.

HEIMLICH, HENRY J., and MILTON H. UHLEY. "The Heimlich Maneuver." *Clinical Symposia* 31, no. 3 (1979): 3–32.

HODGKIN, JOHN E., ed. *Chronic Obstructive Pulmonary Disease: Current Concepts in Diagnosis and Comprehensive Care.* Park Ridge, Ill.: American College of Chest Physicians, 1979.

———, OSCAR J. BALCHUM, IRVING KASS, EDWARD M. GLASER, WILLIAM F. MILLER, ALBERT HAAS, D. BARRY SHAW, PHILIP KIMBEL, and THOMAS L. PETTY. "Chronic Obstructive Airway Diseases: Current Concepts in Diagnosis and Comprehensive Care." *Journal of the American Medical Association* 232 (June 23, 1975): 1243–60.

———, F. G. ZORN, and G. L. CONNORS, eds. *Pulmonary Rehabilitation: Guidelines to Success.* Boston: Butterworth Publishers, 1984.

KELLING, JAMES S., KINGMAN P. STROHL, ROBERT L. SMITH, and MURRAY D. ALTOSE. "Physician Knowledge in the Use of Canister Nebulizers." *Chest* 83 (April 1983): 612–14.

MATTHAY, RICHARD A. "Foreword." *Medical Clinics of North America* 65 (May 1981): 453–55.

NEWHOUSE, MICHAEL T. "Proper Use of Metered-Dose Inhalers." *BronkoScope* Vol. II, no. 2 (July 1983): 6–7.

Nocturnal Oxygen Therapy Trial Group. "Continuous or Nocturnal Oxygen Therapy in Hypoxemic Chronic Obstructive Lung Disease: A Clinical Trial." *Annals of Internal Medicine* 93 (September 1980): 391–98.

PETTY, THOMAS L. *Prescribing Home Oxygen for COPD.* New York: Thieme-Stratton, 1983.

——— and REUBEN M. CHERNIACK. "Comprehensive Care of COPD." *Clinical Notes on Respiratory Diseases* 20 (Winter 1981): 3–12.

——— and LOUISE M. NETT. "Quality of Life for the Chronic Lung Disease Patient." *American Lung Association Bulletin* 67 (January/February 1981): 5–8.

——— and LOUISE M. NETT. *Enjoying Life with Emphysema.* Philadelphia: Lea & Febiger, 1984.

SAHN, STEVEN A., LOUISE M. NETT, and THOMAS L. PETTY. "Ten Year Follow-Up of a Comprehensive Rehabilitation Program for Severe COPD." *Chest* 77 (February 1980) Supplement: 311–14.

SHEPPARD, DEAN. "Adverse Pulmonary Effects of Air Pollution." *Immunology and Allergy Practice* (February 1984): 25–35.

SNIDER, GORDON L. "Conference Summary" (26th Aspen Lung Conference). *Chest* 85 (June 1984) Supplement: 84S–89S.

YAGER, JEAN A., HERMAN ELLMAN, and MAURICIO J. DULFANO. "Human Ciliary Beat Frequency at Three Levels of the Tracheobronchial Tree." *American Review of Respiratory Disease* 121 (1980): 661–65.

ZISKIND, MORTON M. "Occupational Pulmonary Disease." *Clinical Symposia* 30, no. 4 (1978): 2–32.

COPD AND SMOKING

AACP Subcommittee on Smoking in the Physician's Workshop (Edward R. Munnell, Chairman). "The Management of Smoking in the Physician's 'Workshop.'" *Chest* 82 (September 1982): 359–61.

BODE, FREDERICK R., "Axioms on Smoking and the Respiratory Tract." *Hospital Medicine* (November 1978): 35–55.

CROFTON, JOHN, I. A. CAMPBELL, P. V. COLE, J. A. R. FRIEND, P. D. OLDHAM, V. H. SPRINGETT, G. BERRY, and MARTIN RAW. "Comparison of Four Methods of Smoking Withdrawal in Patients with Smoking Related Diseases." *British Medical Journal* 286 (February 19, 1983): 595–97.

DOYLE, NANCY C. "Even at Work, Second-Hand Smoke Can Affect Your Lungs." *American Lung Association Bulletin,* Vol. 66 (June 1980): 5–7.

HUNNINGHAKE, G., J. GADEK, and R. CRYSTAL. "Smoke Attracts Polymorphonuclear Leukocytes to Lung." *Chest* 77 (February 1980) Supplement: 273.

LUOTO, JOANNE, "Reducing the Health Consequences of Smoking: A Progress Report." *Public Health Reports* 98 (January/February 1983): 34–39.

National Cancer Institute. *Calling It Quits: The Latest Advice on How to Give Up Cigarettes.* U.S. Department of Health, Education, and Welfare Publication No. (NIH) 79-1824.

———. *Clearing the Air: A Guide to Quitting Smoking.* U.S. Department of Health, Education, and Welfare Publication No. (NIH) 78-1647.

———. *Helping Smokers Quit: A Guide for Physicians.* U.S. Department of Health, Education, and Welfare Publication No. (NIH) 78-1825.

REPACE, JAMES L., and ALFRED H. LOWREY. "Indoor Air Pollution, Tobacco Smoke, and Public Health." *Science* 208 (May 2, 1980): 464–72.

SHAMAN, DIANA. "Nonsmokers Make Good Risks, Say Insurance Companies." *American Lung Association Bulletin* 68 (September/October 1982): 2–6.

"Showdown on Smoking." *Newsweek,* June 6, 1983, pp. 60–67.

WHITE, JAMES R., and HERMAN F. FROEB. "Small-Airways Dysfunction in Nonsmokers Chronically Exposed to Tobacco Smoke." *New England Journal of Medicine* 302 (March 27, 1980): 720–23.

DIET AND NUTRITION

American Lung Association. "Juggle Your Diet to Include Carotene." *American Lung Association Bulletin* 69 (May/June 1983): 13–15.

ARORA, NARINDER S., and DUDLEY F. ROCHESTER. "Respiratory Muscle Strength and Maximal Voluntary Ventilation in Undernourished Patients." *American Review of Respiratory Disease* 126 (July 1982): 5–8.

BANTLE, JOHN P., DAWN C. LAINE, GAY W. CASTLE, J. WILLIAM THOMAS, BYRON J. HOOGWERF, and FREDERICK C. GOETZ. "Postprandial Glucose and Insulin Responses to Meals Containing Different Carbohydrates in Normal and Diabetic Subjects." *New England Journal of Medicine* 309 (July 7, 1983): 7–12.

Bowes and Church's Food Values of Portions Commonly Used. 13th ed., revised by Jean A. T. Pennington and Helen Nichols Church. Philadelphia: J. B. Lippincott Company, 1980.

BROWN, STEPHEN E., and RICHARD W. LIGHT. "When COPD Patients Are Malnourished." *Journal of Respiratory Diseases* (May 1983): 36–50.

BROWNELL, KELLY D. *Behavior Therapy for Weight Control: A Treatment Manual.* Philadelphia: University of Pennsylvania, 1979.

BUNKER, MARY LOUISE, and MARGARET MCWILLIAMS. "Caffeine Content of Common Beverages." *Journal of the American Dietetic Association* 74 (January 1979): 28–32.

DRIVER, ALBERT G., MERLE T. MCALEVY, and JACK L. SMITH. "Nutritional Assessment of Patients with Chronic Obstructive Pulmonary Disease and Acute Respiratory Failure." *Chest* 82 (November 1982): 568–71.

EVANS, MARGUERITE, and JOHANNA DWYER. "Diet, Nutrition and Cancer: A Summary." *Cancer Institute Bulletin* 3 (Spring 1983): 2–3.

GOLDIN, BARRY, and SHERWOOD GORBACH. "The Relationship between Diet and Breast and Colon Cancer." *Cancer Institute Bulletin* 3 (Spring 1983): 4–5.

KATCH, FRANK I., and WILLIAM D. MCARDLE. *Nutrition, Weight Control, and Exercise.* Philadelphia: Lea & Febiger, 1983.

KUO, PETER T. "Hyperlipoproteinemia and Atherosclerosis: Dietary Intervention." *American Journal of Medicine* 74 (May 23, 1983): 15–18.

MAYER, JEAN. Introduction. *Cancer Institute Bulletin* 3 (Spring 1983): 1–2.

MCCAULEY, KATHLEEN, and TERRI E. WEAVER. "Cardiac and Pulmonary Diseases: Nutritional Implications." *Nursing Clinics of North America* 18 (March 1983): 86–96.

OPENBRIER, DIANA R., MARGARET M. IRWIN, ROBERT M. ROGERS, GARY P. GOTTLIEB, JAMES H. DAUBER, DAVID H. VAN THIEL, and BERNARD E. PENNOCK. "Nutritional Status and Lung Function in Patients with Emphysema and Chronic Bronchitis." *Chest* 83 (January 1983): 17–22.

POWER, LAWRENCE. "Diet and Blood Cholesterol: The Important Role of Specific Fibers." *Physician & Patient,* May 1983: 46–52.

SELIVANOV, VAL, GEORGE F. SHELDON, and GARY FANTINI. "Nutrition's Role in Averting Respiratory Failure." *Journal of Respiratory Diseases* (September 1983): 29–32.

THELLE, DAG S., EGIL ARNESEN, and OLAV H. FØRDE. "The Tromsø Heart Study: Does Coffee Raise Serum Cholesterol?" *New England Journal of Medicine* (June 16, 1983): 1454–57.

Veterans Administration, Medical District 1. *Nutritional Care Guidelines for Allied Health Services.* Vocational Rehabilitation Therapy Graphic Arts Clinic, Rehabilitation Medicine Service, Veterans Administration Medical Center, Northampton, Mass.

EXERCISE

COCKROFT, A. E., M. J. SAUNDERS, and G. BERRY. "Randomised Controlled Trial of Rehabilitation in Chronic Respiratory Disability." *Thorax* 36 (1981): 200–3.

DEGRE, S., J. SOBOLSKI, and C. DEGRE-COUSTRY. "Controversial Aspects of Physical Training in Patients with COPD." *Practical Cardiology* (January 1979): 37–45.

JONES, NORMAN L. "Exercise Testing in Pulmonary Evaluation: Rationale, Methods and the Normal Respiratory Response to Exercise." *Medical Intelligence* 293 (September 11, 1975): 541–44.

MCARDLE, WILLIAM D., FRANK I. KATCH, and VICTOR L. KATCH. *Exercise Physiology: Energy, Nutrition, and Human Performance.* Philadelphia: Lea & Febiger, 1981.

SICILIAN, LEONARD. "Mechanisms and Management of Exercise-Induced Asthma." *Practical Cardiology* 9 (August 1983): 143–52.

SINCLAIR, D. J. M., and C. G. INGRAM. "Controlled Trial of Supervised Exercise Training in Chronic Bronchitis." *British Medical Journal* (February 23, 1980): 519–21.

SONNE, LEONARD J. "Inspiratory Resistive Training in Patients with Severe COPD." *BronkoScope,* Vol. II (April 1983): 2–3.

————, and JAMES A. DAVIS. "Increased Exercise Performance in Patients with Severe COPD Following Inspiratory Resistive Training." *Chest* 81 (April 1982): 436–39.

STEIN, DAVID A., BERNARD L. BRADLEY, and WARREN C. MILLER. "Mechanisms of Oxygen Effects on Exercise in Patients with Chronic Obstructive Pulmonary Disease." *Chest* 81 (January 1982): 6–10.

PSYCHE

DUDLEY, DONALD L., EDWARD M. GLASER, BETTY N. JORGENSON, and DANIEL L. LOGAN. "Psychosocial Concomitants to Rehabilitation in Chronic Obstructive Pulmonary Disease." Part 1: "Psychosocial and Psychological Considerations." *Chest* 77 (March 1980): 413–20.

DUDLEY, DONALD L. "Psychosocial Concomitants to Rehabilitation in Chronic Obstructive Pulmonary Disease." Part 2: "Psychosocial Treatment." *Chest* 77 (April 1980): 544–51.

MCSWEENY, A. JOHN, ROBERT K. HEATON, IGOR GRANT, DAVID

CUGELL, NORMAN SOLLIDAY, and RICHARD TIMMS. "Chronic Obstructive Pulmonary Disease: Socioemotional Adjustment and Life Quality." *Chest* 77 (February 1980) Supplement: 309–11.

SEX

BAUCOM, DONALD H., and JEFFREY A. HOFFMAN. "Common Mistakes Spouses Make in Communicating." *Medical Aspects of Human Sexuality* 17 (November 1983): 203–19.

BRAUER, ALAN P., and DONNA BRAUER. *How You and Your Lover Can Give Each Other Hours of Extended Sexual Orgasm.* New York: Warner Books, 1983, pp. 64–67.

KAPLAN, HELEN S. "Sexual Relationships in Middle-Age." *Physician & Patient* Vol. II, No. 10 (October 1983): 11–20.

KIERAN, JAMES, with NAN PHEATT. "No End to Love." *American Lung Association Bulletin* 67 (December 1981): 10–13.

KRAVETZ, HOWARD M. "Sex and COPD: Counseling That Allays Patients' Anxieties." *Consultant* (July 1982).

———. "Sexual Counseling for the COPD Patient." *Clinical Challenge in Cardiopulmonary Medicine,* Vol. 4, no. 1 (June 1982): 1–5.

———, ANNE M. GARLAND, DAVE HARNER, and CAROL HARNER. *A Visit with Helen: A Summary for the Patient.* Slide-tape Presentation for Patient Education, Pulmonary Foundation, 1011 Ruth Street, Prescott, Arizona 86301.

———, LILLIE WEISS, and ROSALYN MEADOWS. *A Visit with Harry: A Summary for the Patient.* 1981. Slide-Tape Presentation for Patient Education, Pulmonary Foundation, 1011 Ruth Street, Prescott, Arizona 86301.

NOEHREN, THEODORE H., "Editorial Comment." *Clinical Challenge in Cardiopulmonary Medicine* 4 (June 1982): 5–6.

COE

ASLETT, DON. *Is There Life After Housework?* Cincinnati: Writer's Digest Books, 1981.

CARNEY, ROBERT M. "Clinical Applications of Relaxation Training." *Hospital Practice* (July 1983): 83–94.

LAPUC, PAUL. Relaxation Exercises. Northampton, Mass.: privately recorded, 1982.

ROHAN, WILLIAM. Relaxation Exercises. Northampton, Mass.: privately recorded, 1983.

RECREATION

COPPOLILLO, HENRY P. "The Value of Recreation." *Physician & Patient,* Vol. I (September 1982): 66–68.

GONG, HENRY, JR. "Advising COPD Patients About Commercial Air Travel." *Journal of Respiratory Diseases,* Vol. 5, no. 6 (June 1984): 28–39.

Index

MYRA B. SHAYEVITZ, M.D., F.C.C.P.

Graduate, Barnard College, 1956
Graduate, New York University College of Medicine, 1959
Diplomate, American Board of Internal Medicine
Member, American College of Physicians
Fellow, American College of Chest Physicians
Director, Pulmonary Medicine, Respiratory Therapy and Cardio-Pulmonary Laboratory, Veterans Administration Medical Center, Northampton, Massachusetts
Cochairman, Cardio-Pulmonary Fitness Program, VAMC, Northampton, Massachusetts

BERTON R. SHAYEVITZ, M.D.

Graduate, Cornell University, 1953
Graduate, New York University College of Medicine, 1957
Diplomate, American Board of Internal Medicine
Life Member, American College of Physicians
Director, Intensive Care Unit, Veterans Administration Medical Center, Northampton, Massachusetts
Cochairman, Cardio-Pulmonary Fitness Program, VAMC, Northampton, Massachusetts

Drs. Myra and Berton Shayevitz work at the Veterans Administration Medical Center, Northampton, Massachusetts. Dr. Berton Shayevitz is the Director, Intensive Care Unit, and Dr. Myra Shayevitz is the Director, Pulmonary Medicine, Respiratory Therapy, and Cardio-Pulmonary Laboratory.

Together they chair the Medical Center's Cardio-Pulmonary Fitness Program.